neurosculpting

neurosculpting

A Whole-Brain Approach
to Heal Trauma,
Rewrite Limiting Beliefs,
and Find Wholeness

Lisa Wimberger

SOUNDS TRUE
BOULDER, COLORADO

Sounds True
Boulder, CO 80306

Published 2014

Cover design by Jennifer Miles
Book design by Beth Skelley

"Angel" and "Castles Made of Sand" written by Jimi Hendrix © Experience Hendrix
LLC. Used by Permission/All Rights Reserved

Printed in the United States of America
Library of Congress Cataloging-in-Publication Data
Wimberger, Lisa, 1969–
  Neurosculpting : a whole-brain approach to heal trauma, rewrite limiting beliefs, and
find wholeness / Lisa Wimberger.
     pages cm
  Includes bibliographical references and index.
  ISBN 978-1-62203-228-0
  1. Meditation—Therapeutic use. 2. Meditation—Health aspects. 3. Post-traumatic
stress disorder—Treatment. 4. Psychic trauma—Treatment. I. Title.
  RC489.M43W557 2014
  616.89›14--dc23
                                    2014025548

Ebook ISBN 978-1-62203-458-1

10 9 8 7 6 5 4 3 2

For my mother, Jean,
July 26, 1934–October 29, 2013.
May you continue to teach me how to BE.
And for my father, Edward,
whose strength and resilience have astounded me.

To be great, be whole;
Exclude nothing, exaggerate nothing that is not you.
Be whole in everything. Put all you are
Into the smallest thing you do.
So, in each lake, the moon shines with splendor
Because it blooms up above.

FERNANDO PESSOA, *Poems of Fernando Pessoa*

contents

contents

acknowledgments

No amount of thanks is enough for the many people who helped create the magical moments that have shaped me, and this content. Havana and Gilly, the loves of my life, thank you both for helping me go through the best and worst moments of my life during this magical and sometimes difficult process. I have also been blessed to use the techniques outlined in this book to journey through massive healing and transformation with my brother, Kurt. It's been amazing to be in this together. A special and deep thanks to Nathan Josephs, my partner in crime on many levels; your friendship has meant the world to me, and my family. The list that follows is, of course, a feeble attempt to recognize the gifts I've been given by a great many individuals. Thank you Haven Iverson, Amber Taufen, Shanti Medina, Alicia Fall, ALL of my NSI-certified facilitators, and the supportive and powerful folks at Sounds True.

introduction

death doesn't get the last word

Imagine a normal and uneventful morning where in the midst of washing your face, your life disappeared without warning, along with everyone you loved. I've flirted with and dated death since I was fifteen years old, when I had my first near-death experience in the bathroom at my parents' house. Of course, I didn't know then that I had a seizure condition that caused me to flatline. I only had an inexplicable, mystical, and painful episode that left me confused and blown open. I had fainted before, but this time was different. I remember standing at the sink, looking at myself in the mirror, and wondering why my face suddenly appeared to be melting. The room quickly closed in on me while I desperately tried to hold on to the counter top. I heard a distant voice say, "oh no" as if it came from someone else. And suddenly I was in another space where I was fully conscious yet completely unaware that my body was on the floor. In that other consciousness I had a vivid encounter with Zahara, a mystical female force I'd never forget—one who visited me often in later episodes and who would help shape the rest of my life. I came to know her as The Mother. I don't know how long I lay on the floor that day listening to her as she told me about neurons and the galaxy. Eventually a faraway buzzing sound grew closer and louder, crushing my ears and shooting pins and needles through each cell of my body. There was nowhere I could retreat to, no pain-free area of my body, no space of clarity in my mind in which I could find shelter.

I prayed for it to stop.

Just underneath that deafening sound-feeling came the whisper of my own moaning. When I opened my eyes, I could see the brown tile underneath the counter. To look elsewhere but straight ahead was a nauseating vertigo nightmare. What happened? Why couldn't I move? How was it possible to feel stuck to the floor as though a great force pinned me down?

I was in a puddle from head to toe and wondered if I had urinated. The floor tile on my face was cold. Cold was good. That's all my clouded mind could grasp. I was embarrassed for my family to come home and find me, so I hoped they didn't. An indescribably long time later I managed to crawl to my room and fall asleep without anyone knowing what happened. I'd keep this a secret for a long time.

I was a very healthy teenager who exercised, didn't smoke cigarettes, never drank alcohol or experimented with drugs. What could possibly be happening to me? Years later, I learned that my vagus nerve, which is responsible for regulating breathing and heart rate in the medulla of the brain stem, had triggered a very primitive response we all experience sometimes: the freeze response. You know those moments of fear when you hold your breath and remain silent? This is your body engaging in a normal freeze response. Mine, far beyond the normal spectrum, dropped my heart rate so rapidly that it stopped beating. This caused blood and oxygen to be in short supply to my brain. So my brain did what it's supposed to do in those cases and shut down all cognitive processes. In other words, my cortex and cognitive functions turned off. One minute I was there, the next I was gone.

This continued to happen for the next twenty-five years: a few more times in bathrooms, some of them at my parents', others at my own home as I got older. One time in my twenties, I regained consciousness with my head wedged between the toilet base and the wall, my legs bent awkwardly under the claw-foot tub. When I was finally able to stand and look in the mirror I noticed a black eye from hitting my face on the windowsill on the way down. Later, in my thirties, I had an episode during a doctor's exam and awoke to a needle of atropine, or liquid adrenaline, ready to plunge into my heart. I got my actual diagnosis that day: I had a seizure and flatlined. My heart stopped long enough for the nurse to run to the next room, load the needle with atropine, and come back. I had gone into the doctor's office that day for a routine exam and I left with the news that I had a condition. I now had a story that helped me make sense of the most confusing pieces of my life.

Yet another time I seized and flatlined in a food court in front of my three-year-old daughter. I was unconscious long enough for the paramedics to arrive. They helped me, but of course could do nothing for the emotional scars that this caused my little girl. When I was coming to, I heard her ask the paramedics in her tiny little voice if mommy died.

My worst seizure was when I was almost forty. My husband found me unconscious and crumpled in the corner of the kitchen with my eyes fixed and unblinking and my body rigid. He prompted me to breathe over and over again each time I stopped. I remember feeling the ease with which silence takes over when there's no breath and no heartbeat. I remember hearing myself bargaining to survive—one self saying I should die for good, the other arguing to stay. My husband kept his hand on my chest for what seemed like forever, and he lovingly crawled with me in slow motion all the way up the stairs to our bedroom, inch by excruciating inch.

These are only a handful of times out of the many episodes that snuck up on me out of thin air and whisked everything away. In these moments of silent heart and mind I've experienced a consciousness that has a life of its own—one that seemed to inform the path I'd eventually take in life. Each of these blackouts fully engaged me in an alternate reality I perceived was real, including waking up with visceral memories of events I swore I was engaged in while I was actually unconscious. Fortunately, these alternate narratives gave me vital information through metaphor and storyline, which I never once took for granted. For example, the first day I experienced Zahara, The Mother, during my first blackout, was the day she taught me the importance of neurons as they relate to my ability to communicate and to heal myself.

Because some of us learn best through facts, and others of us learn best through allegory, I was well aware that my visions in these states were as important as what I might learn in a waking logic state. They seemed to be breadcrumb trails to the gateways of my wholeness.

I have spent most of my life navigating these episodes, searching for the cause and the cure, trying to glean meaning that would somehow justify the trauma I felt, and the damage I perceived I did to my daughter's sense of safety in the world. These events shaped my life in powerful ways and led me to learn about my brain's neurology and my central nervous system's wiring. In all of that research and self-exploration I found a way to rise above my conscious and subconscious limitations. I experienced a way to use a whole-brained approach to heal my trauma, rewrite my limiting beliefs, and live from a place of wholeness. This book is the fulfillment of a promise I made to myself to share this powerful work with you in the hopes of empowering those of you on the edge of physical, mental, or emotional collapse.

Although I wrestled with the concept of death as a very real and imminent option for far too long, I am not unique. Death is a very imminent option for you as well, but for the most part, we don't think about it that way. I'll bet you don't normally think the next bite of lunch will be your last or that the magazine you're reading in the bathroom may be the last thing you ever see. You probably don't focus on the fact that this may be the very last sentence you ever read. Instead, we easily drift into the illusion that we have the next minute, the next hour, and even tomorrow. We plan for events in the future with excitement in the belief that we will be alive to see them come to fruition. This is a gift that keeps us moving forward, and it can also be a hindrance that causes us to go about our days as an automaton and without reverence. What if you didn't have the illusion of tomorrow to hold on to? What if today was your very last day? How would you live your life differently? Would you step bravely into your wholeness?

I lost longevity's grand illusion long ago. In losing that I easily steeped and festered in the grip of fear, anticipating the worst could happen at any moment. We can lock into the search and avoidance of fear and get stuck in a negative loop. This makes us contract around opportunities, too afraid to take risks that may lead to mistakes and pain. Maybe this sounds familiar to you. Maybe you are someone who can't help but prepare for the worst, always. I spent a long while functioning like this.

But my otherworldly experiences, visions, and meditations informed me of another option: to see in the mind's eye that life is temporary and fleeting, and to use that lens to extract the juice out of every moment with gratitude as though it were the very last. I have learned to make the most of life because I know it is not a dress rehearsal. This belief or story liberates me, opens me up to possibilities, and gives rise to opportunities of expansion. This belief demands I savor each moment and interaction. This belief causes me to choose forgiveness and compassion over judgment and punishment. I'm hoping over the course of this book you discover what's possible when you revere each of life's moments.

As the founder and creator of what I term the Neurosculpting modality, I have marveled at the gifts these life experiences have afforded me. I am committed to helping individuals find a way to move out of fear, rewrite their limiting stories, and savor more of life. I have taught these techniques to first responders since 2007 as a way for them to deal with their daily stress and long-term post-traumatic stress disorders. I am honored to be a civilian who has the unique opportunity to go into the depths of a police agency's pain and emotional vulnerability and help guide them to lasting healing. I've taught this powerful technique to individuals from the CIA, FBI, Secret Service, the U.S. Military, and Homeland Security. I have a private practice teaching those who are stuck in the grip of limitation and fear. Because this work can benefit the masses, I created the Neurosculpting Institute as a place where people could learn how to transform their lives. This often involves introductory experiences, in-depth curricula about neuroplasticity, nutrition, and hands-on meditation exercises. Those who benefit from Neurosculpting get a comprehensive package of exercises and tools for daily use. I've created a place where science and mindfulness come together in full support of mind, body, and spirit healing. It's a place where people come to learn how to embody spirit, understand their physiology, extract more from life, learn how to give from their highest self, integrate their fractured selves, and be agents of change in their own lives. We accomplish this without dogma or formal religion, welcoming all.

The analytical side of me always wanted to put a reason to things. I wanted to find a cause-and-effect relationship for events in my life and to find comfort in thinking I *knew* something. The mystical side of me always wanted permission to not care about a cause-and-effect relationship or a logical reason for things. It just wanted to *be*.

My experiences, seizures, and visions showed me that until I found a way to merge the analytical, science-based side of me with the experiential, intuitive, and fantastical side, there would always be a one-sided approach to life. Worse, that one-sided approach would always be in conflict with the opposing and silenced part that had no permission to express itself. I already knew life was too short and too rich to allow for this type of limited existence. I will offer you that same opportunity in this book to access both the analytical side and the fantastical side to find out what they both have to offer in your pursuit of healing and wholeness. The visionary journeys I describe at the beginning of each chapter are an opportunity for accessing the metaphorical content informing the science-based studies I engaged in.

So what fresh perspective could a regular person like me offer to a timeless exploration of head versus heart, body versus spirit? Surely, if I were a guru or political leader, I'd come in as a heavyweight, right? My status or credentials might give my insights extra value or credence in your mind. I want to be as forthright with you as possible because I believe we are establishing a relationship through this work. I have no intention of pretending to be a scientist, doctor, therapist, or any other "ist."

I believe this journey we take *together* offers you something quite special. We begin on a level playing field. From that space, I have the opportunity to converse with you as I ponder some of the big questions and possibilities presented in this book. Generally, I like to ask lots of questions, which has made me a great student. I present many of them here for you to think about, but I may not always offer answers. We'll explore topics ranging from mental illness to unconditional love to death, and many things in between. Perhaps it is our collective job to derive answers that work best for us. Maybe those are yet to be discovered.

I *am* a teacher at my core, not because I am an expert, but because I know the best way to learn, synthesize, and integrate is to share what I know so others create their own relationships with that information. As *you* reflect the information shared, *I* gain a deeper understanding. So, you see, I *need* you to find your own way through all of this in order for each of us to understand it more deeply. It is imperative that you question areas of this text, that you take threads of content and go off on your own journey of education and experience, and that you allow content that feels right to you to embed and grow roots in your life. In this way we are synergistic, symbiotic in our application of this information. This is how we create a ripple effect. As this book explores what it means to live in a common language between heart and head, I begin to relate to you differently. You then explore these same ideas and relate to your world differently. Only together can we make lasting change and shift everything.

Some teachings foster a leader-follower relationship, which I person-ally find disempowering for everyone. It's easy to fall into a passive role and not do the work if all you have to do is follow someone who has. I had a very uncomfortable and interesting experience once in having to fire a student for this very thing. This student was nice enough, and seemed very interested in applying neurosculpting to rewriting some of her patterns. We worked together for a little more than a year. She came to each session with copious notes about what she observed in her life. She took notes throughout each session. She learned techniques in our private sessions, attended many of my workshops—sometimes twice—and seemed very eager for change. I began to notice that although she spent time in learning sessions with me, there were very few changes in her behavior. At first I began to feel like maybe I wasn't teaching her very well. Soon I began to receive emails asking for special treatment, extra attention, and discounts or free sessions. At this point I asked how much she was using the many tools I had taught her.

Her answer was that she was not. At that point I had to admit that I could assist no further. As I am not a therapist, it felt as though the teacher-student relationship had shifted in a direction of co-dependence. Her life was still a mess by her own definition. She was well-equipped with acute observation, but she hadn't applied *any* of the practices. Observations only go so far, and then one must choose if they are truly ready to change their patterns. In my opinion, cultivating the actual practice is possibly more important than spending years adding layers to our self-reflections. In the spirit of empowerment I am giving you a platform upon which to create a practice of your very own.

I created Neurosculpting out of my own limitations with the many meditation and energetic modalities I'd learned. I perceived some of those teachings to be very one-sided, engaging only pieces of my whole self. I have been meditating since I was a young child. I used meditation for many things: relaxation, coping, healing, exploration, and fun. But as an adult, after decades of a meditation practice with great teachers, I felt like I hit a plateau. Shouldn't life be much different by now? Much richer? Much more neutral? More magical? Shouldn't I have a handle on my gripping fears that seemed to be the trigger for my seizures? Yet my life still felt as if I was just holding on, effort-fully attempting to be joyous, barely coping with some of my darkest stories. Why wasn't I allowed to be my analytical self in meditation? Why wasn't I allowed to be my intuitive self in my corporate job? Why did I have to compartmentalize pieces of me like hushed children wanting to be heard?

So I dove deeper into my studies of the brain and medical neuroscience.

Huge pieces of this puzzle fell into place as I learned of the mind's relationship to my thoughts and nervous system. (I use "mind" and "brain" synonymously, although I recognize a great debate in this area.) I realized that perhaps I was still in my infancy when it came to meditation; that maybe others could access healing I couldn't because they started from a different place. It was time to take some big steps backwards and stumble right into this design called Neurosculpting.

WHAT IS NEUROSCULPTING?

Neurosculpting is a mental training process that quiets our fight-or-flight center and activates our prefrontal cortex, which is the mind's seat of our compassion and empathy. It also engages left- and right-brain stimulation and incorporates a somatic awareness for a whole-brain and whole-body approach to meditation and rewiring. It's a lifestyle of day-to-day exercises, nutritional tenets, and meditations designed to allow dialogue between the compartmentalized and silenced parts of ourselves. It involves learning about a brain-supportive diet, exercising, identifying and enhancing opportunities for neuroplasticity throughout your day, and practicing regular meditations for mental training. The benefits of this regimen are deep and long-lasting. Neurosculpting contributes to increased cognitive functioning, reduces emotional and physical stress, supports a healthy immune system and a reduction in inflammation, increases growth hormones in the brain by way of exercise, stimulates creativity, supports mood regulation, and creates a ripe platform for creating new beliefs.

It is a practice that takes commitment, and a commitment that takes practice.

This lifestyle practice helps individuals identify and create a ripe environment for the brain to drop its old stories and prime it to believe a new and better story or belief about oneself. Our inherent gifts of neuroplasticity showed me that I could program or encode stories or beliefs much better if I primed myself with nutrition, mental dynamics, and the right exercises before trying to tell the new story. And what if that story involved the union of mind, body, and spirit? We'll explore this idea much more in our time together.

This practice is the thread that sutures together mind, body, and spirit, allowing us to live more fully and in a more integrated way than we have before. Just as language has a grammatical structure and syntax that provides us a foundation from which to express our most amorphous and slippery thoughts, I needed a foundation—a language—that could help communicate my most spiritually expansive desires and experiences in a way that made sense through the body-world in which I live. I was tired of separating and isolating amazing magical moments of awe and expansion as though I could only have those if I were off on some retreat, far away from the daily grind of my life.

The meta-structure of Neurosculpting provided far more than I ever thought possible. My episodes of seizures and flatlining disappeared. At that point, I knew I had to share all of this with anyone who would listen and participate.

HOW TO MAKE THE MOST OF THIS BOOK

Because I was trained as an educator, I present this information in a way that offers you opportunities to make it your own and to perhaps create a study guide. Perhaps you're like me in believing two halves of the brain are better than one. In that spirit, I've begun most of the chapters with some of my meditational experiences, which may engage the experiential side of your brain. While reading these you may feel appeasement for that fantastical side of you. You may find these sections help you get lost in vivid narrative or evoke emotional responses. They don't follow any rules of logic or evidence-based reality. They are simply what occurred either during my episodes or in my deep meditations. I present them for those of you who want to know more about the visions that have driven my approach to this work and for those of you who want encouragement to explore your own dreams. For those of you wanting a new way to access information about your own life, these visions demonstrate how that can happen. The snippets I've chosen for you are some of the ones that have informed my life's deepest healing.

If you don't connect with the narrative descriptions of my experiences, then feel free to skip the introductory segments and move on to the more logically organized content that might support your analysis-based self better. These sections will challenge you to evaluate current beliefs as you compare them to new scientific discoveries. You may find these sections concretely define more about the way the mind works and how our belief systems are neurologically created and supported. These sections give you resources for further education and science-based self-examination.

Orienting to the Content

Whether you find your way in to this work through the experience and feeling of the content, or through the meaning and evidence of the text, you will find opportunities to reflect upon the mind's ability to rewrite old patterns and create new ones. Together we'll explore the concept of free will and what it means to us individually and neurologically. We'll dive into the basic premise behind neuroplasticity and its relationship to our personal empowerment. We'll focus on how to cultivate a more self-nurturing relationship and create new self-care patterns as a foundation for self-love. You'll have a chance to challenge yourself into radical self-acceptance and you'll also have opportunities to ponder the idea of contentment and being enough. You'll walk down memory lane as I present information about how memory formation is critical to our ability to heal and grow. You'll make your own decisions about the challenge mental illness presents to spiritual expansion and the way in which your small or large traumas can inform your own growth. Together we'll talk about the challenging path of hope and forgiveness in the face of conflict, and even explore the meaning we can extract from death. Lastly, we'll spend some time together looking at the balance of love versus fear in bringing us to a place of healing, acceptance, and wholeness.

I suggest using a special journal or notebook to accompany your reading. There will be many places in this work that ask you to write down your own thoughts in a personal discovery journal, do an exercise, or create your own mantras. These Discovery Journal exercises are clearly labeled in each chapter and provided for you in the hope that you engage with the information in a personal way.

Each chapter ends with a Putting It All Together exercise as a way to bring this information into your day-to-day life. I will give you prompts to begin a dialogue with others, or make notes in the margins. I will give suggestions for how to personalize this and even take this into your community. At the end of the book I'll give you a template for a daily regimen that includes meditation exercises and a few resource sections covering Brain Basics 101, Inquiry Exercises, and some Weekly Brain Changers. By doing all the journal and integration exercises, you will create your own personalized manual by the time you finish this book.

The most vital part of this work is the part you take away. Each of us learns and experiences differently. Some of us savor the words and meanings, some of us connect emotionally and pay more attention to how the content makes us feel rather than what it means. Some of us get vivid mental imagery to help us define our experience, while others sense something greater and inexplicable coming through the words. I may intend and hope for a lot of things, but none of them are as relevant to your needs as your own interpretation of this content.

So I'd like to invite you to participate in this as we explore the thread weaving mind, body, and spirit into an experience of healing and wholeness. As you become acquainted with the possibilities of Neurosculpting, you may decide you want a very concrete tutorial and walk-through of some specific meditations. You can access those through two powerful audio companion programs that take you through many guided meditations and practices: *Neurosculpting for Stress Relief: Four Practices to Change Your Brain and Your Life* (Sounds True, 2014) and *Neurosculpting: A Step-by-Step Program to Change Your Brain and Transform Your Life* (Sounds True, 2014).

Knowing you will take your own story from these words, I will note my intentions nonetheless, in case you find parallels.

- I intend for this work to cause you to question your own limiting beliefs.

- I intend for this work to empower you to create the life you want.

- I intend for this work to be a conversation and not a monologue.

- I intend for this work to help you suture mind, body, and spirit.

- I intend for this work to be both your companion and your practice.

- I intend for this work to be a mirror for you to look at yourself with nonjudgment.

- I intend for this work to become a ripple effect of positive transformation.

- I intend for this work to help your head and heart speak the same language.

- I intend for this work to help you heighten the two-way communication between body and mind.

- I intend for this work to open doors of deeper consciousness.

- I intend for this work to be your lifeline in the face of all that is inevitable.

- I intend for this work to increase your access to ease and grace.

- I intend for this work to have its own relationship with you outside of my intentions.

1

a quest for free will

And so castles made of sand melts into the sea, eventually.

JIMI HENDRIX, "Castles Made of Sand"

I was at the entrance of a quaint garden, slowly opening the creaky wooden gate to what looked like a cottage, vibrantly colored against a backdrop of space and stars. There was lush greenery and a lawn full of mushrooms. A small dark figure walked out of the cottage, approaching me although it had no feet to touch the ground. One moment he was there, at the door, and the next he was directly in front of me, close enough for me to see the riveted seams of his black leather face. Had I ever encountered Anubis (the Egyptian God of the afterlife), I imagine he'd look similar. The small creature's lupine face was not at all threatening. It was mostly welcoming and expectant, as he told me they'd been waiting for me. I didn't know how I got here, but I knew this was where I was supposed to be.

He said we had much to cover and very little time. With a touch of his hand on my head, we were suddenly in front of a council of elders sitting stoically at a long table in a bright and sparsely furnished room. They all resembled my gracious guide, exhibiting varying degrees of blacks and browns on their faces. They spoke only to him. He translated their high-frequency sounds. I was to learn of the two parallel histories, both of which he told me were my own. He said that on Earth, we are born with ego, and that for us it is important to use that to cultivate the idea of independent survival for a few early years until we can stand on our own. But as humans, we forget to drop it, choosing instead to believe all of our lives that we are separate from each other and in competition. He told me that this limits our potential and our sense of freedom, and keeps us small as we spend too much energy in a conflict based on an us-and-them view of the world. The council unanimously emanated a frequency in unison. My guide paused, responded in kind, then nodded to them before speaking to me again.

"I will now reveal important information to you. I will show you a more expansive way—our way. The way to freedom."

He placed his hand on the back of my head and showed me pictures and experiences as though I had grown up with them. Without any memories, I seemed to remember that as a child in his care, I was born without ego, experiencing complete unity with those around me. Oneness vibrated through me, and I saw that each face of my childhood was a reflection of me. There was nothing I could do to another that I didn't feel and experience myself. My heart was bigger, flushing warm waves of contentment with each beat. There seemed to be no filter between each breath and my implicit trust in my own safety. In this unity experience, there was no fear. He flashed me forward to age twelve, the time for a rite of passage where one becomes acquainted with his or her own ego. With oneness in every fiber of my being, the introduction of ego was nothing more than a vehicle by which to discern my personal contributions to the larger organism. It was not a limiting force or a veil of illusion. It was something we only used when we wanted to give more to the whole and ourselves. From a base of unity, our egos functioned like sparkle on an already beautiful picture; it was just a small texture adding one tiny layer of depth to an already infinite source. As his child, I saw my most expansive self, free of the limiting stories my human ego had so diligently invested in. He told me that in his world we all had seats at the table of the divine, and if I could learn how to shed my stories and learn to **be** differently, then I'd remember all of this and once again know my own freedom.

VACATION MIND

If I told you that you could learn to squeeze the vibrance and beauty out of each moment of your life, strip away those limiting stories, and experience more joy, ease, presence, and freedom in your life, would you care what effort it took to do that? Would you say yes to a new daily practice that promised to get you there? We have the ability to dismantle our mental fortresses and prisons. Our beliefs shape themselves based on our experiences, molded and sculpted by our engagement with life. They can just as easily reshape themselves when the waves of life change our direction suddenly. Our beliefs are our castles made of sand, seemingly solid until the waves of change wash in. I have come to believe that Neurosculpting is the power that can direct those waves and help us rebuild our thoughts.

I'm sure you know the incredible release that happens when you are nearing a vacation you've been planning, especially if it's one you've been thinking of for a long time. For those of us in the daily grind of a traditional work/life relationship, this may be a vacation we've planned for and worked an entire year or even years toward. Maybe you relish the moments that lead up to that one- or two-week paradise, perhaps even adopting an "I don't care so much" attitude to normal stressors as you get closer to the moment in which you know you will leave it all behind. Suddenly, maybe that co-worker's complaint isn't such a bother in your mind. Maybe that dog next door who barks too early in the morning or too late into the night doesn't seem to set you off as much. I remember that in my last few months as a public school teacher I was a better teacher than in all the months of my career before that. I was relaxed, found more joy, had more patience, and connected more personally with the children.

Why? Because I saw a light at the end of the tunnel that shifted the present moment into a different perspective. I was navigating the present moment differently, which gave me a sense of freedom and empowerment. Suddenly, as in my vision, I didn't feel stuck in the old story of who I was. My mind happily engaged in the full potential of what life could be. I had access to more of me.

Remember yourself on your favorite vacation. Did you feel that sense of openness and potential? Did you feel like a freer version of yourself when the routine of your day no longer mattered?

Sometimes after a vacation, we carry that relaxed mentality back with us for a short time after we return. Or sometimes we might feel sadness the day our vacation ends, as though that experience is now on a shelf, unable to bleed into our mundane experiences of the "real world." Vacation has shown me how large an influence my mindset is on how my body chooses to experience and express itself in the world. I smile more on vacation; my muscles relax; and my aches and pains recede. In fact, I wear different clothes and adopt a different posture when I'm on vacation. I wear my body differently, and it experiences the world differently based on some minor circumstantial changes like location and schedule.

What makes our vacation self so expansive, joyful, and full of permission? What strips us of that when a random day printed on the calendar notes the end of the vacation? What invisible constraints do we shed and then put back on during that whole process? What underlying processes or behavior scripts shift our body relationships in the world from one context to the next? It is clear to me when I think about this scenario that my mind, body, and spirit are in one sort of communication *before* vacation and in a different type of communication *during* vacation. The catalyst for this changing communication might just be our beliefs, illusions, and expectations.

As we prepare for that long-awaited vacation we take the set of beliefs we call "day-to-day" and store them away, reaching for a special set of beliefs we call "time off." Our daily beliefs and stories might prime us to be burdened with deadlines and relentless to-do lists. These beliefs might limit what we think we are allowed to do in an eight-hour chunk of our day. They can define our responsibilities, permissions for leisure, and forgiveness for indulgence. These daily beliefs also carry with them judgments around what type of vehicle we drive, where we live, and even what sort of recreation we are allowed to have. Maybe in our day-to-day lives, we don't allow ourselves to eat dessert for breakfast or have a glass of wine with lunch. Maybe there is a type of protocol in our brain that says that sort of thing is not appropriate *unless* we have a valid excuse. Does your set of day-to-day scripts give you permission to nap during the day when you want? These daily beliefs dictate where we go, when we go, how we get there, what we wear when we're there, and how we feel about ourselves. How much more could you learn about yourself if you were aware of these subtle scripts? What freedoms might you experience if you could adapt the stories of who you are and release the version of yourself your ego had created? Who could you be without those scripts? What might be possible?

As we shift from the set of daily underlying beliefs to our special-edition vacation beliefs, we might change how we prioritize our time and what activities we choose to engage in. What special permissions do you give yourself when you are on vacation? You may find yourself interacting with people differently. Perhaps you engage in activities you'd never dreamed of except during vacation. You may no longer become annoyed at things that typically bother you. You may not feel compelled to answer the phone to take a certain call that might normally make you interrupt the important thing you're doing.

I always wanted to know why people were more likeable, gregarious, funny, happy, and even radiant during vacation. It couldn't be *just* the destination; it had to be a shift inside.

WHAT'S BEHIND THE RESCRIPTING?

This shift is not restricted to vacation; we experience these types of permission shifts in relation to the people we spend time with, the geographic location we find ourselves in, and the availability of certain opportunities and resources. Maybe you notice you use a different script with your best childhood friend than with your new colleague. Or maybe you find yourself animated in a completely different way when you are talking with a sibling versus a bank teller. We act differently when we're out on the town than when we're home with the family. We take different liberties when we have an abundance of money versus very little. We change what drives us when we have a job we care about versus a job we hate.

Aren't we actually toggling between different scripts constantly? Does your language and tone change when you take off your work clothes and put on your gym outfit? Do you have different social permissions when spending time with your child versus your best friend? Although we don't spend much conscious time thinking about all the rules that correspond to each, we have cultivated an intimate relationship with each of these scripts in order to implicitly and automatically access all of their rules and behave accordingly.

. . . .

DISCOVERY JOURNAL noticing your guiding scripts

Make two columns down a page in your journal, naming one "Daily Permission Scripts" and the other "Vacation" or "Weekend Permission Scripts." Note in your journal some of your daily permission scripts around food, sleep patterns, and recreation during your work week. Example: "I don't eat breakfast during the work week because it doesn't fit into my commute schedule" or "I don't go out dancing or to the movies during the week because . . . " Next, note some of your permission scripts around these same topics as they relate to your weekends or even vacation time. Observe some of your own sets of permission scripts. Note the differences that you slip in and out of with very little effort or consciousness.

How much energy does it take to create and store all of these different life rules? What is that shift inside that causes us to harmonize our mind, body, and spirit differently from one situation to the next? Maybe neuroplasticity can give us some clues.

NEUROPLASTICITY AND FREE WILL

When I think of neuroplasticity and the brain, I can't help but feel giddy. We are so fortunate to live in the age of the brain, when science has put these amazing neural machines of ours at the forefront of research and discovery. We know so little about how the brain works, yet the pace of our discoveries about its processes is speeding up exponentially. Our basic understanding of what these machines do on a cellular level has made it possible for us to feel more in charge of our destiny and well-being than ever before. We are at an exciting time in history where alliances between researchers are happening on a global scale—all in an attempt to create a working brain model.

Although many of these scientists use their understanding of the brain to postulate that we don't really have free will, my experiences and research have shown me that without a doubt we *do* have free will. More importantly, I want *you* to believe that you have free will in the same way my vision with the lupine creature communicated it to me. With this one belief comes autonomy, empowerment, and a proactive approach to life and freedom. This is how we begin to change our daily scripts and drink more of life's juice. This is how we move into wholeness. In fact, this die-hard belief in free will is a foundational model for Neurosculpting.

Neuroplasticity is the idea that although we once thought the brain was fixed in its anatomical function and structure, it's actually adaptable. We are not dealt an unchangeable hand. At one point, our mental capacity was considered finite. It was believed that brain cells, or neurons, died and could not be replaced. We believed, based on science, that dysfunctions of the mind were stamped as our destiny and that we had no ability to change that. We believed that damage was permanent. With the discovery of neuroplasticity comes the realization that we, and science, were wrong. We are infinite in capacity instead!

Thanks to the work of scientists like David Hubel and Torsten Wiesel in the latter half of the last century, we know that the brain is much more elastic and resilient, malleable and trainable than we once thought.[1] We know that we can birth new brain cells in the hippocampus, an area of the brain highly involved in our ability to create and store memories. Those new brain stem cells can then migrate to other areas of the brain for specified differentiation, becoming functional cells where we need them.[2] This implies our own ability to repair, regenerate, and enliven our own minds well into old age. In other words, we can regenerate cognitive functions in our senior years. Abilities lost to stroke damage can migrate to other areas of the brain. Neural maps or control centers of certain bodily functions can be taken over by neighboring real estate when damage occurs.[3] This means that damage to an area can be compensated and adopted by another area. For instance, damage to an area of the brain that controls one finger may not mean the permanent loss of finger control as the neighboring area may be able to gain those abilities. Areas of cognitive abilities can also migrate from areas of damage to areas of healthy tissue. This current model of the brain has vast implications for healing damage due to physical, emotional, and mental stressors. Through this model, we no longer have to feel destined for senility and dementia, and we can look forward to the potential that our senior years can be rich, engaging, and mentally stimulating.

What neuroplasticity has illuminated for us is the miracle that we call "learning." The process of learning neurologically looks a bit like our brain cells following a specific process: activating with electrical excitation; firing their neurotransmitters, or chemical messengers; sending signals across a gap; reaching and connecting with other neurons through dendrites, or spiny branches; and signaling the next neuron.[4] These cells chemically and electrically signal each other when we learn new skills. For instance, when I pay focused attention to a new skill or activity like salsa dancing, rock climbing, or learning a new language, I have an excitatory response in brand-new neural maps, which then encode that new information. I'm learning something new, and my focused attention allows this experience to stick so I can retrieve it again later and build upon my skills.

We have the ability to strengthen neurological activity in some areas and lessen activity in others, growing and diminishing skills and competence all the time. Sometimes this happens unconsciously, and other times this happens when we exercise a skill with intention. Each skill and thought we have is associated with an electrical firing in the brain that creates a path of activity. Imagine you are walking through the dense woods for the very first time. You may expect that the forest floor is full of leaves and vines, maybe even a bit difficult to navigate. You might find yourself stumbling for balance and a clear foothold. But each time you return to that forest, you retrace your steps and walk the same path to get you from point A to point B. What will happen to that path over time? How much more easily will you find that path after having walked it for years? And what happens to the alternative path you tried to make just once but never revisited? How easy will it be to find that one year later? Strengthening and diminishing neural activity in the brain is similar.

Sometimes we're relearning old lessons like how to tie our shoes, repeating the same thing for the hundredth time, and this neurological process is happening in an already established map or path. Consider the idea of reinforcement. Perhaps I have a skill or a hobby that I enjoy. Each time I practice that skill, or essentially retrieve that mental script and revisit it, I relearn that skill and store it again, this time with just a little more sticking power.

But this sticking power isn't just true for skills and activities; it is also true of our thoughts. Thoughts have sticking power. What does it mean to you to know that each and every thought we have, no matter how fleeting, is exercising and embedding a neural pathway? My guide showed me in my vision that the more I exercised the belief that I was ego-bound to a competition with others, the more locked up I'd remain in my stance of who I was. He showed me that a new belief about my own identity could open me up to freedom. Which thoughts about yourself did you exercise today?

THOUGHTS: THE MECHANISMS
OF A PREDICTION MACHINE

The brain is a prediction machine; it likes patterns and prefers to default to pattern recognition. This ability enables us to do many things, like focus on a new piece of stimulus while doing something routine or rehearsed. Once our brains know a pattern, the well-rehearsed script of that pattern is filed in an easily accessible way so we don't have to spend all of our resources learning it over and over again. We can access it with little thought and basically automate it. And once it's automated, our brains have resources available to focus on new stimuli.[5] So creating patterns is extremely handy in using our brains efficiently. Imagine how much time you'd spend tying your shoes each day if you hadn't automated the pattern of tying laces. Or think about those who hunt-and-peck on a keyboard versus those who have automated the skill of typing. The hunt-and-peck person will likely use far more energy, thought, and time to type than what the automated typist expends. And to get even more fundamental, think about pattern recognition in small children when they are learning what shapes are and how to fit them into the appropriately shaped holes. Once they learn a shape and its corresponding hole, they'll never get frustrated again as young children (or even as adults) trying to cram a square peg into a round space.

We can use patterns to our advantage, automating physical patterns for improved performance as in sports, or dance, or building the muscle memory for playing an instrument. But what about the process of developing thought patterns? This can be a gift—or it can be a detriment. If we rely on cultivating and honing the patterns that no longer serve us, or the ones that are out of context, then we can become slaves to the past and limit the potential new choices in front of us. Imagine spending all of your neurological resources reinforcing the wrong way to play an instrument, or the cumbersome way to hunt-and-peck on a keyboard. Many of us have automated some negative, limiting, or fear-based thought patterns that might have been true once, but they are no longer true now (or maybe they were never true), yet we're still using them as a way to predict what we expect to experience in the world.

Imagine still being stuck in that "I can't do it" belief you had when you first were learning how to ride a bike. Or maybe you relate to this experience when you consider all of the ways in which you stick to the limiting stories you created of yourself in your youth when you believed you weren't as good as or as deserving as a competitor. You may still be referencing those beliefs when you contemplate making changes in your job, seeking a promotion, or trying something new. So what are some of those thoughts?

· · · · · · · · · · · ·

DISCOVERY JOURNAL expired

Write down some of your fear-based thoughts about the world that you developed years ago from a situation or lifestyle and still believe—even though that same thing has not happened to you since. An example might be that carrying a purse is unsafe because ten years ago yours was stolen. As you list each one, see if you can decide on a realistic expiration date for the event. Maybe it's already expired, and you can imagine it being put to rest. Or maybe you imagine you have a few more months to go before you are comfortable saying it's expired. Just notice your own experience of having to put an end date on some fears that might not serve you any longer.

HIJACKED BY THE LIMBIC SYSTEM

The same neuroplastic process that applies to developing and reinforcing our skills and behaviors also applies to our reliance on certain emotional reactions. Not only do we use patterns to govern our actions, but we also use them to guide and interpret our experiences in life. Let's break down this process of learning and entrainment even further by looking at two areas of the brain that have a very interesting relationship: the limbic system and the prefrontal cortex. The limbic system is considered our fight-or-flight control center regulating our ability to run from danger or fight against threat. It's the part of the brain and nervous system that recognizes a perceived threat on the path in front of us and preconsciously causes us to jump in reaction.[6] It's also involved with regulating basic survival needs such as the pursuit of food, shelter, and the need to procreate. Fortunately, for the survival of our species, when it comes to the fight-or-flight response, this fast-acting system doesn't need for you to ponder or analyze a dangerous threat before you jump. If you came upon a poisonous snake, that delay in reaction time would be the death of you.

Our limbic system, associated with brain and body structures like the hippocampus, amygdalae, hypothalamus, pituitary, orbital prefrontal cortex, and adrenals, orchestrates an evolutionarily refined system of commands and signals so that we intuitively know how to save our own lives in the face of imminent danger. Many of the limbic system's structures exist in the temporal lobe, located toward the midpoint of the brain and spanning both hemispheres.[7] It is our self-preservation command center. And although this is a gift to the survival of the human race, it is a gift that is prone to abuse. It's been exercised so much in each of us for the duration of our existence on this planet that it often thinks it should control more than what's in its "imminent fear" domain. It can easily believe its job is to push you into threat and danger response when you get cut off on the highway, or when you are accidentally overlooked at work as your boss hands out the bonuses. It likes to speak up when your friends forget to invite you to go out with the group or when you are cheated out of something you believe you deserve. It roars loudly in the face of unfairness, and it kicks wildly when we are ignored and dismissed. It proclaims definitively when we are no longer number one. My guide from my vision showed me that my limbic response was at the heart of my biggest ego struggles, causing me to take stances I didn't need to and to fight phantoms that weren't there.

The limbic system has become so efficient that it easily forgets the difference between real threat and perceived threat as it fires up its effortless control of our nervous system's threat response. Imagine how graceful life could be if we developed a skill or language to help this amazing system relax just a bit. What if this system could respond to a pause button or a "not now" statement? What if it could remain dominant when we are in real danger, yet yield to our higher thoughts of forgiveness and compassion when that served us better? Through Neurosculpting, we can create this pause button and give ourselves easy access to this ability, so that we aren't victim to our patterns of reaction.

PAUSE LIVES IN THE PREFRONTAL CORTEX

The potential for pause is there, and it lives in the prefrontal cortex (PFC). The prefrontal cortex is located at the front of the brain, behind the forehead, and pieces of it fold under, reaching back toward the limbic system. There is a unique communication between these two areas.[8] Structures of the prefrontal cortex correlate to some very different attributes of our human expression and experience than the limbic system. Whereas the limbic system governs basic survival needs, the prefrontal cortex is associated with experiences like compassion, forgiveness, big-picture thinking, delayed gratification, understanding social norms, empathy, problem-solving, expressive language, goal-setting, and many other attributes we like to associate with our uniquely human qualities. Although much of the brain is actively involved at all times in the processing of our varied human experiences, these basic generalities for the limbic system and prefrontal cortex have been discovered. We now know that we can detect *more* activity like higher usage of glucose and oxygen and increased electrical activity in the PFC during states of higher-order thought processing and experiences of empathy and compassion, just as there's *more* activity in the limbic system during heightened states of stress and fear.[9]

The PFC is a much newer part of our brain in our human existence, and even in our own lifetime. Science has shown us that we have evolved the PFC to be much larger than in any other time in our history, whereas the limbic system has been fairly consistent throughout this process. In terms of our individual development, we are not born with a robustly functioning PFC as we are with our limbic system. Our PFC doesn't fully mature in each of us until early adulthood. Its capacity in infancy is far from what its capacity will be when we reach the age of twenty-one. It's a much more complex area of the cortex than some of our more primitive brain structures and it processes stimuli more slowly than the limbic system as a result of its complexity. Whereas the limbic system can act preconsciously, the PFC involves conscious processes. It likes to mull concepts over, make logical sense of things, steep in the experience, and project ideas into the future. The PFC can consider the consequences of action, and it can also decide to pause for further examination. This part of the brain has the ability to create the pause button for our more primitive threat response.

And this is where neuroplasticity comes in. We can either keep rehearsing a limbic dynamic in which we are reactionary first, then regret our actions later; or we can begin rehearsing a different dynamic in which the PFC is more frequently exercised and accessed in certain situations in order to create those pause moments. This allows us more conscious choice. As a result, the limbic system can save its resources for when we really need it. In my episode I experienced a sense of empathy and unity with my imaginary community. My spirit guide illuminated the experience of a prefrontal relationship to my surroundings. As a result, I tasted elements of my freedom and empowerment.

When we are intentional about our thought patterns, we can begin to sculpt a neurological firing pattern that favors our preferred dynamic. Think about this example: If you want to learn how to play the guitar you will only do so if you put some conscious intention to it by taking lessons or practicing. You won't learn how to play the guitar if you only hope to but never get a guitar, or strum the strings. In the process of learning how to play the guitar with an intention to do so you will develop the areas of your cortex that involve control of your fingers and dexterity, the associative parts of the brain that connect the image of notes to the sound of strings, and the orchestrated areas that turn mechanical motion into practiced and automatic responses. You've changed the structure of these areas and altered the way they communicate with each other. Our brains respond to exercise and change their function and structure in accordance with how we exercise them. Neurosculpting is the way to create and rehearse this new dynamic.

TAKING CHARGE OF FEAR: FREE WILL AT ITS FINEST!

Taking charge of my unique seizure condition has caused me to believe beyond any doubt that I have free will over some of my subconscious mental patterns or scripts. For almost three decades, my nervous system completely shut down at times of stress or fear. For much of that time, I didn't even know that my seizures were reactions to stress and fear. I thought they were fainting spells. And the triggers for the intense fear were so subconsciously buried that I had no idea what they were. The doctor who held that needle of atropine directly over my heart to resuscitate me helped me take charge of my life by arming me with an explanation. And even though waking up to this experience scared me beyond comprehension, I consider the doctor one of my saviors who gave me my actual diagnosis and started me on my path to recovery—my path to empowerment and choice.

It was the first time I heard the term "vasovagal seizures." My "fainting spells" were actually blackouts and tonic seizures that caused me to flatline on three documented occasions, but it's more like seven by my own estimation. Tonic seizures are the kind in which the body becomes rigid and frozen in a position. Facial expressions become stamped in paralysis as though Medusa just walked by. The ability to remain upright goes away. If you've ever wondered what a rigid sack of one hundred ten pounds of dead weight sounds and looks like hitting the ground, I assure you it's not graceful.

During the hours of recovery on his office table, I found it difficult to want to inhabit a body that could so easily and quickly short-circuit. I had suddenly been thrown into a completely different view of my own history. I was now a woman with seizures who almost died. Apparently, I'd been having them for years. An hour before I arrived in his office, I believed myself to be normal, yet now I had a "condition." This was fuzzy and hard to comprehend, as my mind toggled between trying to make sense of things and trying to give up. I clearly seemed a victim to this condition and appeared to have no free will when it came to these seizures. How could I possibly gain power over an automatic seizure condition? What was my spirit trying to tell me?

I researched this condition as best I could over the years, and what I found were many articles noting that this was simply a severe drop of blood pressure, which could lead to dizziness and potential fainting spells. All of what I researched told me this was not harmful and there was no real treatment. Yet this was not *at all* my experience. My experience was that my nervous system was regularly engaging in a response it was not designed to tolerate at those levels. The episodes that landed me in the hospital and laid me up in bed for days were a major stress on the recovery of my nervous system and extremely harmful to my ability to function. Much of this literature mentioned that extreme emotional distress, perhaps even stress and fear, caused this condition. Ironically, doctors never once told me to find healthy ways to deal with my stress and fear as a means of treatment. They just said there was nothing we could do about it because there wasn't a pill to fix it.

The intensity of my condition far surpassed the normal fainting spells noted in the literature. I began studying the groundbreaking work of Dr. Stephen Porges, who wrote a defining text called *The Polyvagal Theory*. His theory helped me understand that the nervous system has more options than just relax, fight, or flight. Our nervous system can also choose "freeze."

This immobilization response is actually our first survival line of defense as infants. It's a relic of our reptilian brain. In reptiles, it comes in handy to be able to drop the heart rate and reduce the temperature the body radiates. This "playing dead" is a way to escape detection and predators. In humans, it's not so handy. As infants, before we have dexterity, strength, and mobility, we only have the freeze response at our disposal. We know how to freeze before anything else. In fact, it's even theorized now that this response is correlated to Sudden Infant Death Syndrome (SIDS). In other words, if the brain tells a strong enough story, the body will believe it. If we play dead well enough, we may actually die. According to an article in *Pediatrics,* the journal of the American Academy of Pediatrics, "infants who have succumbed to SIDS have been found to have altered sympathovagal balance compared with control infants."[10]

My case matched Dr. Porges's textbook extreme example.

> . . . the adaptive strategy of reptiles is lethal for mam-
> mals. In the defensive world of mammals, it is necessary
> to increase metabolic output to foster fight-or-flight

behaviors. . . . The consequences of reduced oxygen resources also would depress central nervous system function, reduce behavioral complexity and competent execution of complex behaviors, induce unconsciousness, damage vital organs, and finally, if persistent, result in death. (p. 36)

I was on a precipice. I knew that in the recovery after each successive episode it was harder and less appealing to come back to the body-world. In those moments, my recovery was slow, painful, sluggish, and limiting. Those moments left my body totally depleted, weakened beyond the ability to move or even speak. Going from no blood flow back to a pumping heart far exceeded the pain of pins and needles in a foot that's asleep.

I lost pride and gained humility during the many recovery moments in which I failed to control my bowels or keep myself from vomiting. I was humbled, repeatedly, by my inability to walk upright for hours, rallying just to crawl. Imagine having just experienced unity and the promise of my own freedom by a strange creature in a fantastic vision—feeling the expanse of what I contribute to the universal consciousness—and suddenly, I'm moaning and writhing on the floor, an animal in a cage. My worlds were at odds. I was not going to return from the next episode. I was sure of it.

USING MY FREE WILL TO HEAL MYSELF

I had been hijacked by subconscious fear triggers, which acted as the underlying scripts dictating my nervous system's primitive freeze response. I was in a limbic dominance. So here's where free will comes in. I decided there was no way I was about to let my fears get in the way of a long and healthy life with my daughter and husband. I was tired of flatlining, tired of the seizures, and tired of being controlled by subconscious beliefs or scripts that kept me a victim of my own nervous system's dysfunction. I was exhausted from constantly living in fear that at any moment the world would go away before I had a chance to say, "I love you."

So I made a decision, based on the premise of neuroplasticity and pure faith, like I hope you will. I committed to sculpt a new pattern and practice it over and over until it was so ingrained that when that unknown subconscious fear or even extreme stress came into my life, I'd have another option or script for my nervous system to call upon. I didn't need to know what the subconscious fear was. In fact, I may never know. I needed to create an alternative script that enabled me to practice and entrain a new response to the body sensations that signaled me about an imminent seizure. The truth is that we may never consciously know the stories that guide our behavior. But that is not a hindrance to healing because neuroplasticity does not rely on discovering the *why*. It relies on entrainment. What if I chose the fight script I had been rehearsing instead of freeze? After all, that was a realistic and more energy-efficient choice for mammals! Choosing the fight response would allow me to maintain my heart rate in a way that could sustain oxygen to the brain. My brain's oxygenation would then allow me to stay cognitively aware, albeit angrily aware.

I believed that if I could have *some* choice in which fear and stress response to engage, then I could save my life. But since the fear response I was engaging in was a preconscious one, I'd need to do a massive amount of work to create and rehearse a new story well enough for it to be embedded as a new preconscious behavior script. And I'd need my PFC to help me create and rehearse that script.

Each time I was laid up in bed for days, recuperating from an episode, I began to rehearse a new script. This new story involved the same fraction-of-a-second warning in which an episode took over, only in this rehearsal, I chose to fight instead of freeze. I used the power of my PFC to create vivid pictures in my mind's eye that were aimed at a future goal. I layered in lots of creative details as I replayed this story in my mind, over and over, until I could picture and recall each detail of choosing the fight response. I was an actor in a play, and I rehearsed so well that if ever these circumstances of body activation presented themselves again—those brief moments when tunnel vision narrowed my view and I felt light-headed—this new script would flow effortlessly without thought. I intended to act so well that even I'd believe it!

Since my last and worst episode, I've been able to stop three other episodes before they caused the seizure. I hadn't been able to do that in almost thirty years! Yes, science has shown me that subconscious scripts dictate my world, specifically my blackouts, but my spirit has chosen to create a new script that could interrupt the subconscious one. This is the essence of Neurosculpting. It was my spirit's decision to stay in my body longer that gave me the ability to do that. For me, my spirit made the initial decision and my mind executed it. Because of my victory redirecting my own autonomic nervous system response, there's no scientist or set of studies on earth that can take away my sense of free will. And I want *you* to feel this same empowerment.

THE SCIENCE OF FREE WILL

Science has shown that we can expand our "neural reach," or our pathways, so that we can form new connections from one area of the brain to another, and conversely, we can also prune that reach back. Plasticity means that the brain changes second by second with each passing wave of thought, motion, emotion, and experience—just like those castles made of sand. With every retrace of a thought, we reinforce a pathway, and with each departure from the path, we begin to create a new one.

A path can be considered a moment of learning in which we create a memory of an experience. If we revisit that path, then the moment of experience becomes a collection, a journal, then a book, and eventually an anthology of memories built upon each other. As we choose to remember and revisit, we strengthen those moments, and as we neglect them, they can fade away.

Our neurological landscape ebbs and flows, waxes and wanes, as we focus and unfocus on the experience of the moment. And as we can expect, each moment transitions to the next before we know it, shifting that neural landscape yet again. The brain is less of a rocky cliff and more of a sandy beach that sculpts a new shoreline with each movement of the tide. Much of this movement happens underneath our layers of consciousness. Some neuroscientists note that the vast amount of subconscious function driving our behavior is *proof* that we are not creatures of free will; rather we are more like robots acting upon hidden scripts over which we have no control.[11] Sometimes this feels true. When you find yourself unconsciously engaging in the same patterns, same relationships, and same fears, you might relate more to the disempowered definition of the conscious mind. In fact, current neuroscience has shown that our brain's electrical signaling for action readiness happens sometimes 1,000 to 500 milliseconds *before* we have neural activity that corresponds to our *desire* to initiate the action.[12]

This underlies the great debate around free will. If we have activity in relationship to an action *before* we are ever *conscious* of wanting to engage in the action, then our conscious desires are *not* the cause of our actions—something else within us has already made the decision to activate. This means that our concept of how the thought process works could be backwards. For example, if you see a delicious piece of cake on the table, you might believe the thought process goes like this: your desire for the cake causes you to grab for it. According to this research, the process looks more like this: I'm sending a signal to my arm to grab for the cake first, *then* I recognize I have a desire for the cake. This is definitely a tough platform upon which to scream, "No! I absolutely have free will!" And this explanation can easily validate every mistake we repeat for the hundredth time. This may very well be your best excuse for those times when you think, "I just can't stop." But does any of this make you feel empowered or in control of your life?

I don't doubt the science behind any of this. But this is a dismal outlook, if you ask me. I don't want to throw my hands up and proclaim my victimization. I don't want to believe I can't change. I've worked far too hard and swallowed lots of pride to own my mistakes. I don't want to give up my ability to take a leadership seat at my very own table like my vision with the lupine creature showed me I could do. And more than this, I don't want *you* to be a victim, either. Rather than challenge the solid science behind these ideas, I'd rather challenge the *definition* of free will. I'd love for you to challenge that as well. Perhaps we are too limited in how we think about free will.

● ● ● ● ● ● ● ● ● ● ● ●

DISCOVERY JOURNAL
recognizing accomplishments and free will

Note some of the times you can remember accomplishing a goal for yourself, no matter how simple or complex. Note the steps you took to reach that goal. Put a star next to each of the steps you believed were driven by your own free will. After reviewing the behaviors that you perceive represent free will, see if you can come up with your own definition of what free will means to you.

THE SOURCE OF YOUR FREE WILL

From the exercise you might have identified ways in which you drew upon strengths in the face of adversity or obstacles in order to achieve your goals. Maybe these strengths were familiar ones, or maybe you even discovered new ones. As you reflect on the times you've accomplished goals you might note that you had to do some uplifting self-talk to make it through moments of doubt or external criticism. You might have had to be your own cheerleader to keep yourself focused. Maybe you drew upon creative solutions that didn't seem feasible at first but worked to get you results. You might have even surprised yourself at your focus or determination. Where did all of this strength come from? What reserves did you draw upon when the situation presented obstacles? The goal you set for yourself and accomplished was both an intentional and a subconscious design. The intentional part makes use of the strengths we know we have, and the gifts of the PFC. The subconscious desire helps us access strengths that surprise us and defy explanation. What's at the heart of both the conscious and the subconscious desire to motivate yourself to an end result? I propose it's this desire that is an expression of our free will.

My lupine vision helped me understand that if I could find the strength to battle limiting ego-based stories of myself, then I could have access to reserves that opened up my own potential. I learned that my reserves of strength required a deep trust and belief in my innate abilities. This trust seemed to me to be the voice of my truest desires, my will. What do those times feel like for you when you surprise yourself with your against-all-odds accomplishments? To what do you attribute those moments when you prove to yourself you are stronger or greater than what you thought?

My idea of free will isn't limited to just the mechanisms of the brain or simply the readiness for action of a firing neuron. If it were, then I'd have to agree with those scientists who have proved our conscious mind is often last to know. What if our mind *isn't* the acting center and source of our will? What if that center is the spirit? You may have different words for spirit. Maybe you define it as the inexplicable source of strength, or perhaps it's faith in your own resources. Perhaps spirit is your intuition, or your deeper knowing, your inner truth, a wiser and higher self—beyond explanation. Spirit might even be the self-made cheerleader that kicks in right when you need it. If spirit, or this unnameable strength, were the source of free will, then science has yet to collect any measurable data at all to prove or disprove the mechanisms of this design. Perhaps science jumped into the paragraph halfway through and began interpreting as though it were the whole. Imagine how much we miss when we assume each of our thoughts and beliefs is the absolute truth.

Maybe you're like me and believe we each have a spirit that came here for a reason. Maybe our spirit wants us to be free, to feel our freedom, to access our free will. Perhaps it's my spirit's design that fuels my mind's subconscious mechanisms. Perhaps that subconscious activity is, in fact, an undercurrent dialogue or response to my spirit. In the search for mind-body-spirit union, I have come to believe that the more I listen to my spirit, the more I can take either subconscious or conscious action to align with what I'm here to do. This is precisely how I found the strength to rescript my tonic seizures. Theoretically, I should have had no real way to override autonomic nervous system responses from the output of cranial nerve ten. These are preconscious and should defy my desire to control them. But in my desperate search for healing, and my need to be healthy for my family, I found that inexplicable strength which was my spirit's design. My higher self intended for me to live longer and that drive fueled me in moments of hopelessness. Through my spirit's free will I pushed myself to practice and entrain better scripts and to ultimately rewrite a pattern that was going to kill me. Listening to my spirit helped me focus on solutions rather than succumb to the medical diagnosis that offered no treatment and no cure.

Maybe your experience listening to your own spirit isn't so obvious. What do those moments of listening to your spirit feel like?

. . . .

DISCOVERY JOURNAL how to hear spirit

In your journal, create two columns. Title one "Times I Knew Something in My Gut and Ignored It." Title the other column "Times I Knew Something in My Gut and Followed It." The items that belong in the first column might be defined by those times you did something and found yourself thinking regretfully, "I knew it!" The items that belong in the second column might be defined by those times you acted effortlessly and in a focused manner in spite of obstacles. Note how the items in each column felt to your body. Notice what your thoughts were like during each memory. What list of body sensations or thought patterns can you identify in the comparison?

Science's simple equation of **UNCONSCIOUS PATTERNS AND THOUGHTS + NEURON-ACTION POTENTIAL = ACTION/BEHAVIOR** is missing a piece as far as I'm concerned. The neurosculpting equation might be more like this: **SPIRIT'S DESIGN + UNCONSCIOUS PATTERNS AND THOUGHTS + NEURON-ACTION POTENTIAL = ACTION/BEHAVIOR.**

I'm not pretending that this is a solid scientific hypothesis. But I am suggesting that what science knows and says about our free will is by no means the whole story. I believe that free will is directly related to our gifts of neuroplasticity. The more we know about what the brain needs, the more we can take control over what we're inputting. It makes very simple sense to me.

A long time ago, I began to ask these two questions I'd like for you to ask yourself right now: "What am I inputting that keeps my limbic brain, or fear response, exercised and strong, and my PFC weak and subordinate?" "Would I input different thoughts or patterns if I had a direct line of communication with my highest self, or spirit?"

• • • • • • • • • • • •

DISCOVERY JOURNAL limbic thought patterns

Note some of the thoughts you believe you repeat enough to exercise your threat response more than your ability to pause and reconsider. Examples might be:

- I'm no good at making friends.
- I'm not as smart as . . .
- They're out to get me.

Next, rewrite each of those thoughts in a way that helps reverse that limbic response. Examples might be: I'm overcoming my fear of making friends.

Whether you agree that we are ultimately agents of free will or simply unthinking machines, it is your neuroplasticity—your ability to learn—that has allowed you to formulate *that* opinion. We have a choice. We can take our current understanding of the brain in its admitted infancy and use that knowledge to feel disempowered, enslaved, and batted around by life, or we can take that very same preliminary understanding and use it to create hope and a feeling of ownership over the small time we have in our bodies—knowing that in even ten years, if we are still alive, we will laugh at what we thought we knew.

I believe that with enough practice and observation, we may all become aware of some of those subconscious scripts, or at least become aware enough to create a new relationship those stories have with our bodies. With attention and commitment, we can create change in those underlying stories. If we believe we have both free will and the most powerful mechanism in the universe inside our heads, then we can access more hope, empowerment, and joy in life. We can sculpt ourselves into our own divinity. Practice and dedication become the challenging part. Neurosculpting requires perseverance and resilience; and you have more of that than you might know.

. . . .

PUTTING IT ALL TOGETHER **cultivating presence**

Maybe you'd like to pause to digest some of what you read or relate it to some of your own experiences. A great way to create a deeper relationship with this information is to take key pieces of this chapter and paraphrase them in your journal or to go back and make notes in the margins. If you can, try making those notes with your nondominant hand. This might be challenging at first, but it will get easier over time. You will naturally slow down with the information and steep in it a bit longer while your PFC is paying attention to a novel experience. Another suggestion for neurosculpting this information is to explain it to someone else in your family or community. The act of having to convey it in your own words will deepen your relationship and help embed the information more concretely into your brain. Ask some friends to do the same discovery journal exercises you did and help them rewrite some of their responses.

2

the nature of resilience

The greatest glory in living
lies not in never failing,
but in rising every time we fail.

NELSON MANDELA

A voice called me further, begged me to fall backwards even deeper. It asked me to remember that moment when I was twelve, running in the field with my friends. It pushed me further, to that day at ten in the backyard playing with my brother's friends—feeling the grass beneath my feet, sensing the not-so-distant chill of the fall air. Continuing on to that moment of birth when the light went from comfort to stark, when fluid sounds became sharp and breezy—when an entire existence of symbiotic union cleaved into singularity.

The Mother told me, "This is the moment of your forgetting. In order to heal you must go further still."

So I anchored my body in the chair and sent my spirit through the spiral of space between conception and all I knew before. And there was my room, a beautiful rotunda richly carpeted and sparsely furnished. One soft plush red couch invited me to recline. There were doors all around me, some sealed shut, others slightly ajar. Each one was a channel to another life, an incarnation I was trying to heal, trying to forget each time I remembered. Transparent veils, like plasma screens, hung like streamers from the open ceiling. Each lit up as I walked through it, illuminating snippets of lives transpired, contracts made and broken, details forgotten. I knew this place. Knew the writing desk that waited for me to sit at it in the middle of the room. I recognized the journal I opened, penned with my own hand, chronicling agreements I'd made so that I could be this me in this lifetime. This was my room, the place I come from and return to. This was the place in which I crafted my story based on all the stories I'd crafted before. This was the place in which I'd learn how to erase. I saw a deck of cards, conspicuously incomplete, on the desk next to the journal. Which card was missing? It was my queen card . . . she was gone.

And when the next door in the rotunda opened I dove into the bright light and became lost in a tumble of colors and conversations. It was at least a few hundred years ago and I was dying alone on a street, covered in months' worth of rancid body dirt. A man walked by and stood near me, afraid to approach, queasy from the stench. I didn't recognize him, but in his breast pocket he carried my queen card. I thought of the many moments in that lifetime where I had been left victimized and discarded, where my efforts went unrecognized. At last, I knew where it was. With no breath or voice to speak, I feared he might walk by, and I'd die, once again, powerless.

But something in the dank air caused him to slow down enough to take notice of the faint light in my eyes as I looked at the card. He lingered and eventually found the strength to approach me. He knelt beside me, holding back the urge to gag as he put both of my hands gently onto my chest, one on top of the other, placing the card between them. "Do I know you?" he asked. I was too weak to answer. "Well, no matter," he said, "nobody should die alone." He stayed with me until blinking was like lifting cinderblocks, then his face faded.

I died smiling that day.

When I came back to the rotunda the card was next to my journal. My deck was complete. I retrieved a piece and got back what was mine. I could now hold the full deck and my bigger picture in front of me. I picked up the pen and rewrote the last page, then closed the journal. What could life be like if I were to play it from a full deck? It was time to leave my room and return to my body to integrate what I'd learned.

I came back through conception, selecting new patterns of genetic code. I breathed my first breath after birth, filling my lungs with action. I revisited that field when I was twelve, noticing the smiles on my friends' faces. I was ready to play my queen card.

WHERE DOES RESILIENCE COME FROM?

What experiences give you the clarity and drive to change what you've always done? What inspires you to redefine and rescript that which is predictable? Where do you find strength to dive into the unknown and rise up with integrity? I am sure each of us would describe the source of our own resilience in a unique manner and voice. Maybe yours comes from growing up poor, rich, safe, unsafe, an only child, or the youngest of ten. For those of us who continue on in the face of fear or limitation, we are pulling that resilience from somewhere.

Resilience is that part of us that kicks in when we are at our weakest and convinces us to continue on. It's also that process of self-reassurance and forgiveness we access when we've made a mistake, yet decide to learn and grow from it. My story of growing up as an idealist in a pragmatic family has come with some vivid memories of being outnumbered in my positive beliefs about the world, or about having my point of view dismissed and negated. I never believed there was anything I couldn't do with enough dedication, work, and focus, yet I often heard the contrary. And I also believed in fairy tales and magic. I perceived I had a relationship with angels. I believed that if there was something on this planet I was called to do, then I'd simply be able to do it no matter what the circumstances. I was mostly told that I was unrealistic, naïve, or had my head in the sand. I heard phrases like:

- You can't.
- That's ridiculous.

- You haven't considered the other side of the coin.
- Are you crazy?
- Yeah, sure!
- That's not possible.

At each of these crossroads I stubbornly dug my heels in to my idealistic stance even more, wanting desperately to prove that all my dreams were actually attainable. I wanted to rip off the fear-based blinders I perceived others wore. It amazed me to see those beloved pragmatists in my life try to burst the dream bubbles I kept inflating. I'm sure that was not their intention, but that was my perception. It's exhausting to always be challenged to prove things made out of faith, or to be told not to put faith in something because it hasn't been proved. I seemed to have always been in search of my power—my queen card.

Maybe in your case your resilience and power came in the face of much tougher times. You might have had to find ways to carry on in spite of great physical illness, family trauma or death, emotional instability, or profound social injustice. Regardless of your situation, we all share the commonality that our strength came from a deeper source that chose not to fall victim to the circumstances threatening us.

I learned early on that to cultivate my power I needed to forgo the discussions and quietly pursue actions to attain the things I wanted. This led me to do much on my own, without the desire for others' input. I became good at secretly strategizing and then pouncing quickly. I was a manipulative strategist for the things I wanted, often planning out counter-arguments to imagined objections. Yes, I'd have all the bases covered by the time anyone had an opportunity to shut me down or kill my dream. I was actively writing scripts of empowerment for myself each time I battled and won against the status quo's declaration of limitation.

I remember having a strong desire to go to Europe as a young teenager to get in touch with my family's roots. With lots of luck and legwork I found a school exchange program. It took quite a bit of convincing, but eventually my parents allowed for this one-month experience. I deeply appreciated this opportunity and what it must have taken for my parents to let me go. Europe in the summertime—my world was blown open at sixteen. My soul was on fire tasting all of the new experiences, hearing foreign languages, eating unfamiliar foods, and meeting people who seemed so exotic. I felt completely alive. Many of those experiences are burned into my memory, palpable with only a scent or a word. My prefrontal cortex was engaged as my attention centers focused on each new moment. My brain's growth hormones kicked into high gear and my reward networks flooded with neurotransmitters like dopamine that made me feel on top of the world.[1]

Returning home was a shell shock. I had just gotten a taste of the world, my unleashed capacity, freedom, and of love. I wasn't ready to come home to being treated like a kid. I cried for weeks and was determined to get back there just as soon as I could. I knew my parents hoped I'd be satisfied after this trip, that I had gotten it out of my system. But I hadn't.

So I employed that manipulative strategist in me and went to work. Having learned well how to sidestep their "voice of reason" discussions, I simply chose not to talk about it. Instead, I employed focus and dedication and I got my first job in an ice cream parlor making four dollars an hour. The walk to the ice cream shop took me right past the bank where I opened my own bank account. Each time I got paid my forty-dollar paycheck, I'd deposit it before I even took it home. I literally saved every penny I could for the next couple of years as I finished high school, all the while staying quiet about my plans. I felt as if I was protecting a hidden treasure. I didn't dare risk having my dreams deflated. Upon graduation, when my parents asked what I wanted for a gift, I'm pretty sure they were expecting me to ask for a party, or perhaps a car. I told them I wanted to return to Germany. Of course, they immediately launched into a million reasons why that would simply be impossible. But I had already bought my ticket with two-and-a-half years of ice cream funds and paid for the whole trip, including six weeks of spending money once I was there. I reiterated to them that I wasn't asking, I was informing them. This is the type of resilience and empowered problem-solving I had been developing, albeit a fairly painful type for my parents to deal with. Every time a loved one told me that I couldn't attain a goal, I catalogued the doubt into a file folder in my brain that became a huge fuel collection that would ignite my actions.

It didn't take long for me to realize that the quickest way to drive me to pursue my dreams and attain them was to put up roadblocks and tell me I couldn't. I was a pit bull idealist motivated by the need to prove wrong those who dismissed me. I began to cultivate a sense of empowerment while realizing I was only as victimized as I allowed myself to be. In hindsight, I'm grateful because the result was that I proved to myself that I could reshape my ideas, my future, and my edges.

Being the victim is not only easy, it can be an effortless default mode for many of us. Why me? How could they do this? If only things were different. Each of us knows what it's like to experience these disempowering thoughts. We know well the feeling of having no control over situations and circumstances happening all around us. Maybe we lost a job, got robbed, or have been the target of betrayal. The victim in each of us could remain stuck in self-pity, trying to find a rational explanation to justify that which is unjustifiable. It's precisely in these times, against all rational thinking, that our resilience has an opportunity to kick in and change the story from self-pity to problem-solving. This is the path of empowerment. This is the way for you to find your power card that may be hidden away in some old story of limitation. Just holding my power card, or sense of resilience, changed how I felt about my entire life in that vision where I lay dying. Somehow it made everything all right because I perceived I had a choice in how to interpret the meaning of it all.

So maybe you're like some of our current scientists who say we are unconsciously enslaved by our brain's current abilities and patterns. Or maybe you're like me, someone who takes the facts and runs as fast as she can in the other direction to prove there is another side to that story. Maybe your empowerment card has gone missing, lost in a sea of stories in which you have no power. What if all you had to do was find it and take it back? How would you use your potency?

• • • • • • • • • • •

DISCOVERY JOURNAL the burst bubble

Write down all the times in which you had a dream you wanted to pursue and someone or something burst your bubble, even if that person was YOU! Note the dream, no matter how small; note how you felt when you thought about attaining it; and note how you felt when you resolved to no longer pursue it. At the end of the exercise write down a healing or balancing mantra of your own, or you can use one from the examples provided. You can use these mantras each time you are stuck in victimhood.

Examples of mantras:

- I release attachments to unattained dreams and open up to the infinite possibility ahead of me.
- I am grateful for the lessons of unrealized dreams, and I take that learning to artfully pursue my life's calling.
- I appreciate all of those who I perceive held me back so that I may learn to cultivate perseverance and dedication on my own.
- Each moment of disempowerment is a potent teacher reminding me that my past is not my future.

Sometimes being stuck in our limitations can feel like we're lost in the jungle. And more often than not, this jungle is in our mind. So what do we need to know about the kaleidoscope patterns of our rainbow jungle?

NAVIGATING THE RAINBOW JUNGLE

We have a landscape of neural jungle in our brains. Modern science has given us Brainbow imaging technology, which is a magnificently beautiful way in which to view the networked jungles of brain cells without having to cut into the brain.[2] This method, developed at Harvard University, enables scientists to locally insert a particular sort of DNA into the genome. DNA is the warehouse of genetic code we carry in each cell that holds all the potential of our physical, mental, and even emotional patterns passed down through our lineage. It's the collection of all of our genetic scripts that dictate the color of our eyes, the density of our bones, and even the predisposition to certain behaviors. When certain genes are activated, they are in an active state of expression. In the Brainbow process when this inserted piece of DNA is expressed, some of the cell types become colorful and fluorescent. We can now look at the most colorful and vibrant representations of the brain and get a sense of the dense, rich jungles of thoughts and experiences going on inside our heads. Imagine looking into a transparent body to the mechanisms in the brain pulsing in a neon Technicolor dreamscape—a carnival of confetti thoughts—and then you might have a notion of how utterly fantastic our neural jungle can be.

With more than 30,000 neurons in one cubic millimeter, which is about the size of a pinhead, and more than 100 million synapses in that tiny space, the territory is potentially more vast than the universe.[3] Our neural rainbow jungles look as though they defy navigation and any sense of order, yet somehow they execute billions of electrical computations each second with efficiency and precision far beyond our understanding. This jungle of electric pulsations creates and fuels our dreams, cultivates ideas of who we are, and motivates us to achieve our highest goals. But it also suffocates us quickly under the weight of our darkest fears. This jungle makes room for others to deflate our dreams or lift us up. It's in the heart of this jungle's darkness that we can rise up from the ashes.

And as discussed in chapter 1, neuroplasticity is at the heart of it all.

A DEEPER DIVE INTO OUR NEUROPLASTIC NATURE

Being neuroplastic means you have electrical firing in the brain that just enabled you to read *these* words and translate them into meaning following some sort of well-established pattern that you likely developed as a child when you were learning which sounds went with which letters. This "I know how to read" pathway, or circuitry, you created was clumsy and new at first, which is why it seemed difficult. But with each repetition the firing pattern strengthened and grew more efficient. You exercised a physical structure in the brain—the pathway—and in doing so, you made it stronger, more flexible, and more accessible. You paid attention to the experience of reading and sounding out words, and with practice, you embedded an indelible map in that jungle territory. This map enables you to locate and retrieve the tools you need each time you read something, building upon a skill set already established, adding vocabulary and fluency with each word. By this very moment you've rehearsed that script so much that it's effortless to read, comprehend, and synthesize meaning from arbitrary ink markings of shapes. Being neuroplastic also means that at any point in time if you want or need to learn something new, then all you have to do is pay focused attention to that experience and perhaps start firing up a brand new pathway that can be exercised through repetition until it's a part of the landscape as well.

Fortunately for us, this ability can serve us well into old age. But when it doesn't serve us well and we no longer chart new paths, we become inflexible in our physical brain structure. This can translate into rigidity of thought and disease of the mind. Consider diseases like Alzheimer's, dementia, post-traumatic stress disorder, and senility, and you will get an idea of what happens to us when we are no longer neuroplastic.

WHAT DOES NEUROPLASTICITY
MEAN TO YOUR LIFE?

Let's pretend that you at your current age are suddenly stripped of your gift of neuroplasticity. You get to keep all that you know up to this point, all of your existing skills and capabilities, all of your memories, and even all of your personality traits. This doesn't seem so alarming until you are given a new project at work that requires you to learn a bit of new information about a program you're using. Without your neurological adaptability to create new pathways you would not be able to learn the new program, store the information, and then build upon it to become proficient. Or think about something even simpler: Your phone company just came out with the upgrade to your phone. This new phone has many more features that would make your life and your business dealings easier. But you won't benefit from this because you won't be able to learn the most basic new applications or how to use them. You are no longer able to fire up a new neurological map that associates with new information. Your current state of existence is as promising and as full of potential as it will ever be. You can't go anywhere new in this jungle of yours. Furthermore, any of the skill sets you don't use for a long time would also eventually be lost. Your capacity for growth would be capped and limited for the rest of your life.

But our neurological adaptability, our neuroplasticity, means that you can edit, sculpt, and rewrite those old stories and fears that cripple you precisely at the time in which you are supposed to expand into the fullness of your life. What would it be like to be able to identify a limiting script and simply edit it? What if you could instantly notice a self-sabotage script that prevented you from succeeding at your job and instantly edit it so that you weren't afraid to apply for that promotion? Consider what it would be like to simply file a limiting script away so it remained in the past as an experience you had, but not a script that you needed to stay loyal to? Who would you be then? What might be possible for your life?

Neuroplasticity happens partly as a result of our ability to create new brain cells and maintain existing ones in a healthy state. These brain cells, or neurons, have a branched formation of dendrites that reach out from them; they look like branches of a tree, or clusters of tentacles. The dendrites' job is to gather incoming information like a net and send it to the cell body. If the information or compiled signals are strong enough, the cell body will continue to send that message with an electrical surge down a channel called an axon, across a synaptic gap, and on to the next dendrite waiting to continue passing along the message to other neurons.[4] All together, this system of cells, channels, and branches becomes a communication network where the electrical signaling from one cell can pass through channels and be spread to other areas, inspiring an electrical signal in those other areas as well. Every thought, everything learned, every sensation, is an electric telephone game. The more we signal through a mapped area, the more that mapped area can reach out to other areas with speed, strength of signal, and ease of firing. When we're not neuroplastic, our reach is limited, and sometimes even shrinks.

When we compromise this system, the dysfunction can have far-reaching effects. Distant maps become isolated, unused, or cut off from activity. For instance, using our neural networks in a way that is not synchronized can negatively affect our ability to use those networks correctly in the future. Consider if you studied piano for six months with a teacher you would have begun to develop a network that synchronized your correct fingering of the keys with dexterity, proper posture, and reading musical notation. You would have begun the process of honing that network. Now imagine your teacher quits and you take a break from playing for a while. The next time you go back to play you might have a friend teaching you who teaches you the incorrect way to hold your wrists, and incorrect fingering. If you practice piano that way for a longer time than you practiced the correct way, eventually you'd impair the network that knew the correct way and you'd reconfigure it to have a stronger association with all the wrong ways to play. If you did that enough, after a long while you'd likely have a hard time relearning the correct way to play piano. Learning a skill incorrectly does more harm to neural networks than not learning that skill.

Then there are medical conditions caused by genetics or extreme lifestyle conditions that affect our neuroplasticity and cause great harm. If we think of Alzheimer's, which is the extreme case of losing our gift of neuroplasticity, not only are we incapable of making new memories, but we also lose our ability to know how to navigate our current situation. We may also lose our ability to retrieve the old memories as well. Without our ability to adapt in each moment we lose our sense of where we are on the map of life. Signposts and landmarks no longer make sense, turning us around until we're dizzy and confused. Old paths, now unused, become overgrown and hidden. Our ability to create meaningful relationships with the details of the world simply disappears. We become lost in the jungle.

We don't have to go to the extreme of advanced Alzheimer's to begin to see how important neuroplasticity is to our lives. If we want to continue to create a meaningful relationship between our own being and the world we live in, then rigidity becomes a limitation, and perhaps even a disease.

WHAT DOES RIGIDITY LOOK LIKE? MAYBE A SPIDER CAN HELP US UNDERSTAND

A little girl five years old went on her first family camping trip. The build-up was weeks in the making. She and her family had studied the map of the national forest, plotting out areas where they planned to hike, fish, and put up their tent. They talked about seeing wild animals she had only read about in books. In preparation for this trip she got her very own sleeping bag, new pajamas, and a big-girl backpack. She was so excited that she even slept in the sleeping bag the night before the trip, falling asleep to the new smell and the anticipation of the next day. This was an exciting time when Mom and Dad wouldn't have to go off to work. Their first night at the park was upon them. The day had been rich with new experiences and exciting vistas of wildflowers and mountains. The smell of a campfire was the most unique scent she'd ever experienced. Her first night sleeping in a tent was to be an adventure. She was primed with new experiences to remember this trip for a long time.

During this time, her brain was activated in a particular way as she paid attention to each new stimulus. As she was paying attention she had a synergistic harmony of dopamine, norepinephrine, and acetylcholine in her prefrontal cortex (PFC), all enabling her to minimize distractions, amplify relevant stimuli, and stamp it all in with some glue. She wasn't fearful, and her fight-or-flight center was quiet. Because it had been a good day of exciting firsts, she was engaging her PFC, storing and cataloguing the new information. In performing like this, our PFC has the ability to stamp an experience into a lasting memory.

As everyone was settling in for bed, the little girl excitedly crawled into her sleeping bag, and laid her head on her pillow, only to put her face right down on a big . . . black . . . spider! What do you think she did? What would you have done?

She screamed, jumped out of her sleeping bag, and cried in terror, inconsolable for a long time as Mommy and Daddy assured her the spider was gone.

And how eager do you think she was to get back in her sleeping bag? How quickly would you get back in the sleeping bag?

So in her heightened neuroplastic state of paying attention to an experience and learning new things, she ran into a very emotionally charged fear moment and activated her fight-or-flight center: her limbic response.

In this moment, she mapped the experience of the spider quite strongly into her storehouse of retrievable experiences. As the PFC has the ability to map something with an emotional charge of curiosity and novelty, so the fight-or-flight center has the ability to take over and map something to fear.

Flash forward to when she was fifteen and went to summer camp. The campfire smell was rich in the air reminding her of her first camping trip. It was time to go to bed. This was her first time camping since she was five. What do you think she did before bedtime? You guessed it! She looked at her pillow, and perhaps even used her flashlight to examine the inside of her sleeping bag just to make sure there were no spiders. She retrieved the old story and reinforced its strength by acting upon it as though it were relevant in the present moment. She was in an old map charting a familiar path through her mind jungle.

What do you think she'd do if a tiny hair accidentally brushed her face while she fell asleep?

Flash forward one more time years later to her weekend getaway with her husband. They were in a cabin; they'd just put out their fire and crawled into bed. Can you just imagine what she asked her heroic husband to do?

In this way, the girl is locked into a rigid pattern of fear. It doesn't matter that the fear moment is decades in the past. If it was big enough to cause an indelible mark on the mind map, then it can and will be retrievable, perhaps forever. This map leaves little room for being present in the moment because it's using an outdated lens. And this old lens comes with real and in-the-moment emotions and body responses that make it very confusing to navigate as we hear others tell us to "calm down."

Rather than unconsciously use our power of neuroplasticity to relearn and remap old scripts, why not use it to consciously create better ones?

• • • • • • • • • • • •

➔ **DISCOVERY JOURNAL taking charge of fear moments**

We each have a fear-based trigger that sets us off and leaves us squirming in terror or holding our breath in fright. Note a few of your triggers that have hijacked perfectly good moments. For example, you might note your fear of spiders as it ruined a romantic date, or your superstition about Friday the 13th that might have ruined a perfectly good day. These triggers are usually ones we consider deal-breakers as they completely turn an experience in the opposite direction. Note next to each experience what it would take in that moment to neutralize your reaction. For instance, you might think about what you would have needed someone to say to you to help you through the moment. You could also consider what you would do if your greatest hero were informing you. If you were the girl from the spider story, your story of neutralization might be that you needed to see how small the spider actually was. Perhaps you would have needed to learn about the benefits the spider brings to the ecosystem to view it differently. Maybe you would have found some humor in it if you saw a funny comic strip with a benign spider. You might even want to create a balancing mantra for each situation or use some of the examples below when you are feeling completely hijacked by an old, outdated fear. These could be similar to statements you wished someone could say to you in those moments of fear.

Examples of mantras:

- I recognize that what I feel right now is in response to an old story that's no longer relevant.
- I am safe and in the present moment, and I can let this fear move quickly and gracefully into the past.

THE POWER OF HOPE

Mantras can be very helpful in rewriting brain scripts—but it is also important that we carry a feeling of hope. And what exactly is hope? Isn't hope the thing you hold on to when you want to believe the situation you're in could be different? Isn't it the light you focus on when all else is dark? Perhaps hope is the declaration that our current situation is temporary, changeable, and adaptable. Or maybe it's the idea that *this, too, shall pass.*

Hope is the very opposite of rigidity. It's the promise that our creations born out of the past can change to meet the future in a way that works better to support who we want to be. The very act of hoping means that, on some level, we believe that change is possible.

Think of the opposite: those times when you felt hopeless. Weren't you really feeling resolved to a situation that you perceived was long term or permanent? Practicing and embodying a focus on positive potential is the difference between living in the *I can't* and the *I can.*

I can't keeps us in our rigid and fixed limitation. It sets a precedent of helplessness and holds tight to that as though that is and always will be true. It is the memorial to an outdated idea of our own capability. It spits on the face of our potential as adaptable and resourceful human beings. *I can't* makes you incapable of overcoming your fears. It sets up shop in your limbic response. It keeps you stuck in past proclamations and future worries. It hides your queen card. *I can't* doesn't serve us at all when it comes to real tests of our greatness. That mindset didn't teach you to ride a bike or learn how to swim. It didn't help you birth your child or attain a lofty goal. It didn't cause you to push yourself beyond your comfort level in anything, and it certainly can't claim any glory in your most glowing winning moments.

I can, on the other hand, is an embodiment of neuroplasticity. And it's a testament to deep self-trust—trust in our own adaptability and ingenuity. It sets us up to embrace changes and expand our existing skill set. *I can* means that we trust we will learn, grow, and bend in whatever way possible in order to get the job done. It professes our commitment to welcoming rather than resisting the unknown. It's a reclamation of our power. *I can* reminds us of the abilities of our PFC.

It's easy for the unknown to spark us into a fight-or-flight mentality. When we experience the unknown, we are stepping out of our prediction models—which, when met, give us a little flood of dopamine so we feel good and safe. When we experience uncertainty, we run the risk of our prediction scripts failing. Increasing the risk of failure can make the unknown feel like a threat.[5]

It's far easier to stick with our rigidity and what we know, even if it's painful, than to open to the unknown and lose our ability to predict all outcomes. Some of us thrive on the unknown, but neuroscience is showing that for many of us, it's a threat to our survival to have to deal with uncertainty. In moments of uncertainty we can choose to retreat, protect, hold tight to old patterns, resist, and fight—but with practice we can choose to embrace, welcome, expand, and learn. The first response is a limbic pattern favoring a fight-or-flight survival approach, while the latter is one that puts trust and faith in our inherent gifts of neuroplasticity, which promises that we can grow from new experiences. The dichotomy is that we know what rigidity brings us, and we know that hope lives in the potential of change. So the magic lies in our ability to minimize our threat response in the face of nonthreatening change. And you know from your own experience that the only constant is that everything changes each day of your life.

Have you used some of these phrases in your most hopeless moments?

- I'll never be able to . . .
- She's never coming back.
- It can't be fixed.
- It's broken beyond repair.
- I'll always be alone.
- That's just the way things are.

The very language of hopelessness implies a dismal, unchanging state, which is the exact opposite of neuroplasticity and adaptability. In this way I believe hope is the face of *I can*. Through the act of hoping, we rely on the very essence of our ability to create new thoughts and project those thoughts to future scenarios. We use our neuroplasticity to transcend the current moment and look to the future. We open ourselves up to potential, possibility, and change. The language of hope is the expression of our neuroplastic strength. If you could, wouldn't you want to cultivate your own neuroplasticity by exercising hope? Our everyday language is a great place to start exercising this practice. Where in your life do you notice the language of rigidity? And where do you find the language of hope?

• • • • • • • • • • • • •

DISCOVERY JOURNAL the language of hopelessness

This exercise can be done over the course of a day or two, but it would be better done consistently over a week. If you'd like to create a chart for this because that's easier for you, please do so. Break each day into Morning, Afternoon, and Evening. Taking just a few moments in the late morning, later afternoon, and in the evening just before bed note all the times in which you recall saying things with absolute and rigid language. Do the same on another chart for all the times in which you recall saying things with open and hopeful language. This exercise may help you identify the amount of time and mental language you devote to reinforcing rigidity and hopelessness versus the language of adaptability and potential.

Example of the rigid chart:

RIGIDITY	Morning	Afternoon	Evening
Monday	My work never ends.	I'll never get that promotion.	
Tuesday			I always get stuck with the dishes.
Wednesday			
Thursday			
Friday			
Saturday			
Sunday			

At the end of the exercise write down a healing or balancing mantra of your own or you can use one from the examples provided. You can use these mantras each time you are stuck in hopelessness.

Examples of mantras:

- I acknowledge that my current situation has an end point, even if I can't currently see it.
- Just as other situations have come and gone, so will this one.
- This situation simply defines my current circumstances, but does not define me or my potential.
- As I open to the potential of change, I open to new and innovative solutions.

If you do this often enough, you might also notice patterns emerging. Perhaps you are someone who notices more hopeless language consistently in the late afternoon, when you are tired and hungry, or more hopeful language consistently in the morning after you've had a good night's sleep. If patterns emerge, you can begin to track those to other factors in your life like what and when you're eating, who you are spending time with during those moments, or what activities you are engaged in at the time. This exercise will also give you a good understanding of what thoughts you are feeding, cultivating, and growing.

• • • • • • • • • • • •

DISCOVERY JOURNAL the language of hope

Now that you've identified some patterns and language related to hopelessness, it's time to turn to the dialogue of solutions. In your journal take each of your thoughts from the RIGIDITY chart and write this phrase next to them: "What would it take for this situation to be different?" You might want to do this on a separate piece of paper. You can imagine the ways in which the situation could be different if you had unlimited access to resilience or strength and write those down as though you are describing how your hero would handle that situation. You might imagine yourself as a character who possesses all the strengths you lack and note how that character would handle that. Make sure to use the pronoun "I" even if you are describing what someone else might do. Once you begin exploring this question you are already in the process of shifting from the hopeless victim to a potential problem solver. Don't expect to come up with all the answers right away. Feel free to leave space so you can come back to this list again and again with solutions.

• • • • • • • • • • • • • •

PUTTING IT ALL TOGETHER cultivating resilience

You might choose a yellow highlighter to note some key areas, or you might make notes in the margins. After making notes in the margins, use some of your own thoughts to start some discussions with your friends about their definitions of hope, and share with them ways in which they can begin identifying the language of helplessness in their own lives. You can even have them read your exercises around the language of hopelessness and hope. Lastly, to help involve your more creative side, you can also make a hope collage in which you choose pictures of what could be.

3

balance in the body-world

To keep the body in good health is a duty . . .
otherwise we shall not be able to keep
our mind strong and clear.

THE BUDDHA

I was standing alone in a black void. Zahara, The Mother, came toward me. It was time for her to show me a way to expand beyond my narrow channels of veins and arteries. She told me I could never hope to know my mission until I found a way to inhabit my body-vessel. I thought I knew how to be in my body—wasn't that simply called being a human? She laughed at me indulgently, in the way a mother laughs at a toddler fumbling at a simple task. Like a puppy grabbed by the scruff of the neck, I was quickly carried off to a suddenly visible garden where she promised I'd learn how to plant seeds in my own body so that my spirit could grow roots and become grounded. Where was I if I wasn't in my body?

I was instructed to close my eyes and inhale deeply. A powerful force and a smell not of this world overtook me . . . sweet, like something I remembered from another life. My inhale never stopped as an unending flood of this scent poured deep into my lungs, then down into my intestines, until it pooled at the base of my spine, bulging itself into my presence. I could not exhale. My initial panic of one-way breath subsided as she told me we were in no-time, no-space. So I allowed the filling to continue beyond my bodily capacity.

My root burst open, and a rushing scented river poured out of me and down into the center of the earth. I was tethered in the most liberating way. And suddenly, the scent revealed itself to be mother's milk. I was nourished and safe from the inside out through an inexhaustible source. My body suddenly released pockets of black contractions as they melted out of my body, carried away by this current. Muscles twitched and spasmed as dangerous faces, threatening gestures, and image after image of self-deprecation erupted with volcanic force.

The open steam valve uncoiled my darkest threads, the emesis of my demons. My eyes poured out their stories. My body spread like melting butter. I could not have imagined being this supple, this expansive. She told me that this is what happens when I am safe enough to release my body's hold on my blackest thoughts.

THE ROLE OF THE BODY IN RESHAPING THE MIND

Because neurosculpting is a practice that involves greater understanding of the body's signals as key informants to the mind's patterns, it is important to explore how the body communicates with the world. My vision showed me that every thought I have finds a root in my body and begins to create a long-term pattern of either holding or releasing it. If we are to pursue a holistic way to heal trauma and find wholeness, it's critical we pay attention to what the body experiences from both the mind's commands and the external environment's influence.

I first heard the term *body-world* used in my studies with Ishaya monks in the early '90s. At that time I had been searching for ways in which to calm my anger. My new job as a public school teacher brought on stress and rage I was never prepared for. I felt helpless and like a wild dervish about to spin out of control. I was searching for some way to get a handle on my swelling emotions when I found a flyer for a meditation workshop in Brooklyn. This is where I met and began my four years of studies with the Ishayas. Their teachings and methods were based in transcendental meditation. The training I received opened the doors to a greater understanding and relationship with my own mind as an integral part of my body. I remember thinking, "Body-world? Wow, I wonder how or if my body is experiencing life when I'm not aware of it?" To be honest, this is a convoluted topic like the chicken-and-egg debate. Does the body inform the mind? Does the mind inform the body? Do I begin to relax *because* I planned the vacation, or did I plan the vacation because my body signaled I needed to relax?

Because it is both, wouldn't it be in our best interest to create clear communication between all that the body experiences, all that the mind thinks, and all that the spirit is called to do? Yet we are not taught how to do this in school or through other institutions so we end up inhibiting ourselves from this rich confluence of information. The term "body-world" woke me up to the fact that the body and mind are not separate, but more like two halves of an organism needing desperately to speak the same language. I had grown up hearing that I was more than just a body. And although I believe this to be true, I also believe that my body is more than just a container. It is spirit fleshed out and made real. What would a computer chip be without an interface like a screen for us to interact with it? What would our voice be without lips to form words? What is spirit without the heart and mind to express its desires? What I do to my body, I do to my mind and soul.

For many of us, it is easier to turn one aspect of ourselves off so we only perceive one source of information. It stands to reason that if we favor only one source of information we will become imbalanced. Living only in the mind inhibits our ability to read the environment through our gut instincts. It cuts us off from vital signals from the only interface we have with the outer world. Conversely, favoring a one-way communication from body to mind may lead us to believe we can solve our emotional problems by simply fixing the body. A nip and tuck here and there might at first seem like a cure, but does little to appease the self-critic or boost the self-esteem in the long run.

When we disconnect this two-way information flow, we have trouble understanding how our negative and stressful thoughts could possibly be related to our illnesses. In other words, our bodies manifest the stress and fear from our thoughts and feelings. My own experience with seizures is a prime example of this. During heightened states of stress and fear my body manifested a complete physical response and shut itself off. It's the same reason why stress can manifest old viruses like canker sores or shingles. Note that doctors tell individuals with hypertension to manage their stress, which comes down to an ability to renegotiate the thoughts that produce stress.

THE POWER OF THOUGHTS AND STRESS
TO INFLUENCE THE HPA AXIS

When we have stressful encounters in life, or stressful thoughts that cause worry or fear, we engage a system in the body called the Hypothalamus-Pituitary-Adrenal (HPA) axis. This is the main stress-response system in the body and is an integral part of the limbic fight-or-flight mechanism. This system responds to our perception of stress by activating the hypothalamus in the forebrain to signal the pituitary gland which, in turn, signals the adrenals to produce stress hormones. This is the most direct link between our thoughts and our body's response. Each and every stressor affects us on a neuroendo-crine level. In some animal studies early activation of the HPA axis through stress and trauma seems to sensitize the system to using that response as its preferred, or familiar, response.[1] If stressful thoughts can predispose the endocrine system to certain responses, then what are your own worries doing to your levels of stress hormones?

Over time, chronic elevation of stress hormones is related to increased inflammation in body tissues in joints, the heart, and even the brain. For example, inflamed joints are a hallmark symptom of arthritis. It stands to reason that if stress and fear have the power to signal our hormones, and hormones have a pervasive influence on all body functions, then our thoughts play an integral role in the physical state of the body.

I have witnessed friends in abusive marriages—and the stress of this was enormous. And yet they often had no idea why they kept coming down with various chronic illnesses. I recall from my own life a period of years in my early adulthood in which I felt disempowered, angry, and frustrated. I internalized a lot of my frustrations, choosing silence over direct communication. During this time, I experienced painful TMJ (Temporomandibular Joint Disorder), sometimes so severe I was unable to open my mouth more than half an inch to eat. I separated my emotional state from my body's health and refused to make a connection between my thoughts and my body. It's no wonder that all the massage and chiropractic treatment that I tried had temporary results. I needed to make a "body-world" change.

My first step was to end the bad relationship I was in at the time—and that alone completely healed my jaw! It's so easy for us to ignore our health issues as though they have nothing to indicate about the thought patterns we keep, the relationships we're in, or the circumstances we create.

It turns out we have a structure in our brain to help us interpret the body-mind communication. I have learned from my studies that there is, in fact, an area of the brain called the insula that correlates to giving our bodily experiences an emotional context in order to make sense of them.[2] As body experiences like deep and slow breathing or calm and regular digestion shift, the insula tracks and makes sense of those visceral and motor shifts—helping us get to balance with those changes. The insula also regulates aspects of our self-identity and our social norms, identifying with pain, and even managing aspects of our emotions. This is key in understanding that queasy feeling in the gut may be a signal that our environment is not safe, or that the increase in sweat or heart rate may indicate something about our level of nervousness. From the time we're born we are learning to associate cues from the environment and the body with a perception of the self, our own safety, and the nature of how we interact in the environment. Perhaps there's some deeper relationship going on in your brain when your upcoming annual work review *coincidentally* maps to your upset stomach. And maybe there's some correlation when your upset stomach *preempts* some bad news waiting for you at home.

In other words, there is a profound communication between the body's relationship to the world, our mental disposition, and our spiritual expansion. Use yourself as the prime example for this. How easy is it to sustain your positive mental disposition when you've been diagnosed with a disease or are down and out with the flu? In those moments is it easier to question your spiritual connection than when you're feeling on top of the world? Do you have to wrestle with the "why me?" or "it's unfair" thoughts? And in cases of dire or terminal diagnosis isn't it just a bit easier to let a little doubt creep in about your own level of faith and spiritual ease?

This complex communication between body, mind, and spirit is much more complex than a mental monarchy. If we could understand the secret messages the body-world communicates to the mind, maybe the mind could understand how to support the body-world differently. Many disciplines like ascension meditation, yoga, and tremor release techniques teach about this union. What if we were to adopt this idea as a general way to look at the world? What more could you discover about your own life if you noticed how your thoughts and body interacted and informed each other? What clues are you missing?

• • • • • • • • • • •

DISCOVERY JOURNAL
deciphering thought-body patterns

Each time you are stressed this week, note what your body feels like during those stressed moments. Areas you can focus on include between the eyebrows, the jaw, the throat, the back of the head, the neck, the shoulders, the chest, your breath, the gut, the bowels, the joints, and the lower back. After one week, review this list to find your common body-world patterns of stress translation. You may even be able to identify in this very moment areas of your body you typically notice during stress.

SCHIZOPHRENIA: A NEW WORLD REVEALED

During my teenage years, my cousin was diagnosed with paranoid schizophrenia. This was a very difficult time for his family—and for ours—because none of us knew much about the condition or how to support him when he was first diagnosed. He was a very charismatic boy, musically and physically talented beyond belief. He played all-star sports; maintained perfect grades; played saxophone, drums, piano; and composed as a child for award-winning adult musical showcases. He was engaging, funny, and extremely personable. I remember how he would carry me around the house on his back like a superhero from room to room, with my hands outstretched. My recollection of my cousin before the diagnosis is one of fun, strength, humor, and joy. And then he had his first reported episode.

In his early twenties, he experienced a complete dissociation with reality. He hallucinated and developed a sense that he was the cause for many of the unrelated events happening around him and in the world at large. He heard voices.

I remember the phone call from my aunt. I tried to decipher what my mother's facial expressions and her sporadic interjections of "for God's sake" could mean while she drew long and deep on her cigarette while consoling my aunt. I sat on the stairs, listening and staring as the phone cord stretched to its limits, then coiled back up as she paced nervously.

He was institutionalized on multiple occasions. I felt sad when I visited him and saw that he felt misunderstood and unable to communicate. He used to show me the pictures he drew in the hospital, colorful scratches of abstract chaos. He'd explain each picture as though I should recognize the objects only he could see. He was given electric shock therapy more than once, and he was put on experimental cocktails of drugs to help him function. Work, school, and his social life were changed forever.

Within a very short time, his body-world changed drastically. He was no longer willing or even able to play sports or music. His body twitched with nervous energy, causing him to pace frequently. His physique went from athletic and muscular to soft as he gained weight from the medications and reduced activity. His sleep patterns no longer matched natural circadian rhythms, and his skin became pale.

The most startling shift in his body-world for me was that he could no longer look me in the eyes. Sometimes we don't realize how important eye contact is until it's gone. Perhaps this is a way the soul tries to hide its pain from the outside world. Remember as a very young child when you thought if you didn't see another person, they couldn't see you? Maybe it's like trying to hide in plain sight. I couldn't help but want for him the freedom I experienced in my vision once I let go of my darkest thoughts.

His gaze went *through* things, off into the distance. Eye contact seemed to exacerbate his symptoms, causing him to look around nervously. I had a sense that if I stared long enough, I'd end up chasing his soul until I had it cornered. I'd coax it out and tell him it was okay, but he never seemed to be able to let me. I had a profound understanding that whatever was going on inside, or whatever his *perception* of the outside world was, was creating a body-world shift in his interactions, appearance, and mannerisms. He carried and inhabited his body differently, and therefore, it changed and molded around his new thoughts.

At this time I was diving in deeply to my exploration of formal meditation and the link my thoughts had with my own state of mental and physical health. In my own meditational journey I felt less judgmental and perhaps more willing to see him for his full potential rather than as someone limited. I thought maybe I could help. Years after his first episode, I took him with me for a weekend workshop to study with the Ishaya monks. The two of us had many lucid conversations that weekend, and I noticed a bit of physical relaxation in his posture, and even an ability to sit for long periods of time. I remember feeling that he peeked out for the first time in a long while—but just for a moment. Seeing through his new way of being, even if only for a brief time, caused me to really wonder:

- Were his medications causing his body-world to change, or were his thoughts causing the shift?
- Did the changes in his body-world send feedback to the brain that caused him to perpetuate and even lock into those patterns?
- Could mental balance happen bi-directionally if the body also received physical therapy, touch, or exercise?

These questions gnawed at me. If his world became painful, scary, and lonely and his behavior and body-world reflected that, then eventually, wouldn't his state of isolation just perpetuate the condition of his mind? This actually seems like an obvious observation, yet this type of integrated and holistic mind-body approach is still considered alternative medicine.

Eventually I learned about the work of neuroscientist Michael Merzenich,[3] who pioneered a deeper understanding of how bodily changes cause neurological alterations in brain maps, and confirmed my belief that my cousin's negative mental shift might also be reinforced by his new physical and lifestyle changes and limitations. It seemed his thoughts and body-world were linked in a constant feedback loop wherein the more he physically transformed and shifted patterns, the more his thoughts mirrored that, and vice versa. I had to believe that spending most of his time asleep in a dark basement was inhibiting his functionality, adding to his paranoia, and shrinking his world. I truly believed that he'd fare much better with a walk in the sunshine, perhaps holding someone's hand, than to be reclusive and sedentary. Yet I don't recall physical therapy being included in his healing regimen. I believed the same to be true for myself: the more I had seizures as a response to stress and fear, the more my body entrained to that response. I felt as if I was stuck in my own feedback loop where my thoughts triggered the body response, and the body response reinforced the validity of the thoughts, trapping me in a dysfunctional and painful body.

How does one's physicality change so obviously in a mental condition, yet the physical changes are not treated? How does one lose the ability to touch and connect to others, yet receive no touch therapy or body work? Where was the prescription for the personal trainer, swimming activities, nutritional therapy, massage, acupuncture, yoga, or any other body-centric health regimen? Doctors never changed his diet, incorporating healthy brain- and mood-balancing foods. They never suggested exercise to stimulate endorphins or healthy growth hormones.

When I was a child, I never once thought that those observations about my cousin's physical patterns might be important, or even heard.

But I could never shake the idea that in trying to help him with his mind, the doctors ignored his body. In fact, according to a small pool of recent research, "regular exercise and physical activity is thought to improve both physical and mental health . . . the overall results show that regular exercise can help some individuals with schizophrenia improve their physical and mental health and well-being."[4]

HOW CAN PAIN HEAL PAIN?

When I reflect back, I see that it was about the time of his diagnosis that I read *I Never Promised You a Rose Garden* by Joanne Greenberg, alias Hannah Greene. This was a semi-autobiographical account of a teenage girl's battle with schizophrenia. This book blew open my world and swept me away. I empathized with the main character and felt I understood my cousin better. Frighteningly, I felt the book described a very personally familiar world, too. In the story, there are moments when the main character suffers so much pain and confusion that she self-mutilates. To me, it made perfect sense, and it frightened me. It was absolutely logical to me that a person in such deep internal pain, locked in her mind, would want to cause physical pain to herself, as a distraction, mask, or reminder that there was a body-world involved too. So I began to wonder about the neurological associations that could cause someone to use physical pain to treat mental pain.

I'm not sure I have found the answer to that question, but what I did find out caused me to revere this magical connection between the body and mind even more. It convinced me that segregating the two only allows for half of life's rich story to come through. The union of body, mind, and spirit demands we begin to decipher the language of each. The discoveries around how the mind processes pain reinforced for me that developing a mental entrainment practice that helped me deal with my negative and fear-based stories could perhaps help me mitigate unnecessary pain in my body.

Science has only begun to unfold and actually map certain mind-body relationships. We have now come to an understanding that the very same neurological pathways in the brain that activate during physical pain can also activate with emotional pain.[5] These neurological implications match what you know in your heart to be true: *emotional pain is as real to the mind and body as physical pain.*

Take a moment to remember your worst sense of rejection. Perhaps when you were abandoned, divorced, cheated on, fired, dismissed, negated, kicked out of a group, or even isolated. You can probably imagine the moment clearly. Perhaps you even remember it in granular detail, noting the clothes you wore, where you were, the tone of voice you heard, the smells, the landmarks, or the date and time.

Or maybe you remember the time you disappointed someone you loved and respected so much that they lost all trust in you. Maybe you recall how you felt you wanted to turn back time or disappear. If you were to describe that experience, what are some of the words that come to mind? Maybe *crushed, torn apart, heartbroken, beaten down, destroyed, shattered,* or *numb*? Do you think it's a coincidence that some of the words you might use to describe emotional states overlap as descriptions of physical states?

- Remember when you were so depressed that you lost your appetite?
- Remember when you were so betrayed that you felt like you could vomit?
- Remember when you were so embarrassed that you felt frozen?
- Remember when you were so angry that you began to shake?

Would you categorize these memories as worse pain than a broken arm or sprained ankle? I'll always choose the pain of a bruise, cut, or break over the emotional fear that flashes at the onset of a seizure. In my case, I've forgotten the experience of much of my physical pain, but still cringe at memories of those emotional episodes. And as my vision showed me, it's the release of those dark stories that causes my spiritual expansion. I think of natural childbirth, which was some of the most intense physical pain my body has experienced, as not being one of those moments. But I can remember heartbreak with a far more visceral response. For some of us, we might even agree that emotional pain is more tangible, lasting, and memorable than physical pain. To what extent are your own aches and pains the result of your fear-based emotional stories piggybacking on the body's physical pain path?

• • • • • • • • • • • •

DISCOVERY JOURNAL **emotional versus physical pain**

Choose your own experience of heartache and write down as many adjectives or phrases as you can to describe your entire memory. Place a check mark next to each of the terms that double as descriptions of physical pain. Then choose an experience of physical pain that you think is comparable and note as many descriptions as you can. Compare the lists at the end. You can even notice which list causes you more of a twinge.

So maybe now we are admitting that we describe emotional and physical pain similarly sometimes. And the science community has begun to make connections between the two. But it might still not be entirely clear how the body-world and thought-world are inextricably linked, or how navigating this communion could be helpful in our quest for health and wholeness.

Neurologically, one of the differences between chronic pain and acute pain is that the acute pain path turns *off* the pain signal after a while by activating inhibitory neurons which *stop* the pain signal. Think of it this way: When you are poked with a needle, you experience acute pain in the moment, causing you to yell "Ouch!" A signal of pain is sent through the pain circuitry, which then activates an inhibitory neuron to turn off the pain signal after a short time. This is why the pain goes away quickly.

However, chronic pain like the kind associated with joint pain, arthritis, and other conditions works a bit differently. Chronic pain can *deactivate* the inhibitory neuron so that the pain message does *not* get turned off, remaining *on* indefinitely. Interestingly, an experience of acute pain like a pinprick can *temporarily* turn off the chronic pain path, giving a momentary sense of relief from the chronic pain.[6]

What are the implications of this? If science is now saying that emotional pain triggers the *same* pathway as physical pain, and acute pain can signal chronic pain to temporarily turn it off, then might it be possible that the character in *I Never Promised You a Rose Garden* used the acute pain of self-mutilation to momentarily deaden her emotional pain by turning off the pain signal? If science is indicating this is possible, at least at the neuron network level, then is it possible to regulate the emotional world by manipulating the physical? What could be different about a person's mental healing if the body-world is incorporated as the organ that expresses the mind's state rather than as an unconscious container?

You are not a one-dimensional being whose brain can be separated from the very body that houses it, connects to it, and has a relationship with it. It's imperative to create dialogue between the two in order for each of us to navigate our world with clarity, health, and intention. That dialogue becomes more defined and accessible when one has a rich mind-body-spirit practice in place.

Consider the work of V. S. Ramachandran, who created an effective treatment for phantom-limb syndrome.[7] This syndrome affects some amputees who continue to feel intense pain from a limb that's been removed. They can feel the limb move, twitch, burn, itch, and tense up. Their pain maps, so intensely embedded in their brain, continue to fire electrical activity—even in the absence of a physical stimulus.

Ramachandran recognized that segregation of the mind-body was preventing the medical community from seeing the bigger picture. So he devised a mirror treatment for phantom-limb syndrome in which amputees put their functional limbs in a box with an open top and a mirror dividing it. The mirror faced the functional limb. From the top of the box, patients could look down and perceive two functional limbs. The eyes, seeing an illusion, began to signal a new reality to the existing pain map, which had been reinforcing the thought that the amputated limb was in pain.

But this new reality said there was a healthy and functional limb there, so the pain path diminished. With daily exercise, individuals with phantom-limb syndrome were able to heal by imagining a new story based on an illusion. These stories exerted control over neurological maps that were stuck in their own illusions. Ramachandran layered fiction on top of fiction to create an alternate reality that resulted in structural and functional changes in the brain map. This is precisely how we neurosculpt our worlds. Consider and even take a moment to answer the questions below:

- What physical patterns are you engaging in that potentially reinforce a negative or imbalanced perspective? *slouching*
- What thoughts are you thinking that communicate danger and disease to your own body? *I'm not good enough someone will find out*
- In what ways are you physically numbing to mitigate emotional pain? *getting lost in my head*
- In what ways are you emotionally deadening to mitigate physical pain? *swallowing my feelings glossing over*
- How are you willing to hurt yourself for moments of relief or distraction from what's going on inside? *overeating too much tv and sitting gym into soreness*
- What illusions are you buying? *that I am a fraud and need to hide.*

DISCOVERY JOURNAL
the effect of stress or ease on our choices

Note the ways in which you treat your body during times of ease and the ways in which you treat your body when you're stressed. You might think about how your diet or exercise patterns shift when you are in times of stress. You might also consider how your desire for certain social activities changes based on your stress levels. What coping mechanisms do you find yourself using during times of worry or stress that you wouldn't normally use? Examples might be:

- When I'm at ease, I enjoy extracurricular activities
  and exercise.
- When I'm stressed, I smoke or drink more.

It has been a little more than thirty years since my cousin's diagnosis. I have spent a long time watching from the sidelines, becoming intensely proud of his and his family's adaptability. I marvel at the way he's reintegrated himself into the world. After three decades of medication, group therapy, and vocational programs, he now plays music again, lives on his own, and even went back to school to get a degree. He is the face of strength, perseverance, and courage. His mother has become a role model for depth, compassion, adaptability, and love. I've learned that the dark stories I released in my vision can have a strong hold on my mind and body, cultivating a disease state that holds me captive. It takes courage and faith to let go of the thoughts that define us, whether we define ourselves as schizophrenic, aggressive, depressed, or countless other labels we can identify with. With science in our corner, cheering us on with our gifts of neuroplasticity and pain management, we can perhaps find a level of trust in our ability to reshape our stories in the pursuit of well-being and mind-body-spirit union.

• • • • • • • • • • • • • •

PUTTING IT ALL TOGETHER cultivating body balance

This chapter introduced many new concepts in current neuroscience as they relate to our ability to increase the communication between mind, body, and spirit. There's much to take in. An interesting way in which the brain increases its ability to pay attention in the moment is to do something it wouldn't normally do—to create novelty. To help digest some of the information presented here with even more focused attention try making notes with your nondominant hand in the margins as you go back through some of the key content in this chapter. Another useful way to embed and integrate knowledge is to create a dialogue around it, or an intimate relationship with it. Partner up with a friend or family member and agree to remind each other this week when body language or posture reinforces a contracted or negative thought pattern. Examples of this might be to help each other sit up straight with shoulders back, or remind each other to make eye contact, and breathe more deeply.

cultivating self-nurture

We can never obtain peace in the outer world
until we make peace with ourselves.

His Holiness the 14th DALAI LAMA

My body was tired, depleted. I had trouble falling asleep, or sleeping too much. I saw the world through darkly circled and sunken eyes. And so The Mother asked me to trust her. She asked if I wanted to meet the part of me who had been absent for so long, the one who escaped at night in my dreams and traveled to what she called the Readyverse, the place in which all of the universe's teachings can be experienced in the moment. She told me I'd come face to face with the part of me afraid to return home to a body I'd been ignoring . . . denying. The Mother told me not to judge the moment in which I called her back and looked in the mirror for the first time. She assured me I'd have the courage to just observe and notice. I felt like a baby bird whose mother prepared to push her out of the nest. I both loved and feared Zahara.

I braced, breathed, and became as neutral as I could. My ether-self came into view and shyly approached, looking much like me from a distance. And when she got close enough, I began to cry as her hopeful yet heavy eyes pleaded with me. She was sallow and parched. She was like the bark of a bleached birch, peeling and cracked. She was hollowed in the throat and gut, a shell of what a person should be.

Her shoulders curled over into a protective hunch. Her lips, split and scabbed, tried to smile a grin of broken gray teeth. Her hair fell out in clumps, lying in thinly curled wisps marking the wake of her approach. Ribs poked through her skin, and her elbows and knees were simply too big for her tiny limbs. She paused, then wheezed as she tried to say my name . . . our name.

How could I have done this to her? How could I expect to live richly when I seemed to be wasting away on the spirit side?

The Mother said I could rebuild it all, but I had to start with what was in front of me. She looked at me with my own sunken eyes and signaled that it was time. So I did what I knew The Mother would do. I tore my ether-self apart, dismembering so that I could remember. Like a rabid dog, I stripped her of her skin and bones, her muscles and organs, until all that was left was one tiny cell buzzing gently with the very first DNA of my existence. I breathed into it with the colors and textures of strength, vibrance, and health. Like blowing a freshly smoldering coal coaxing a fire to burst forth, I blew light into that cell until it glowed brighter than my eyes could see. This cell divided and became a heart, then lungs, then a brain, and then all the other organs in the body. I breathed into her a robust circulatory system and stitched together a bionic skeleton of muscles and bones. I filled her with blood as rich as the earth, and charged her up with care only I could provide.

She began to stand tall. Her shoulders pulled back and her skin brightened. Her hair grew lush and long and her eyes sparkled. Her smile enraptured me.

I looked at the most beautiful self I'd ever known and felt remorse for having seen her on her deathbed. I would never ignore her again.

She turned her back to me and paused just in front of my body where I stood. Stepping back, she overlayed herself onto me, sinking into my body, bleeding herself through my skin and bones. She rushed through my veins and lit up the inside of my brain. She anchored herself into my joints and filled all of my empty spaces. I brought myself back to life in the Readyverse.

BUILDING BLOCKS OF SELF-CARE

My vision of a neglected and worn-out self helped me identify key ways in which my real-time body was crying out for self-care. Maybe, like me, you are a very busy person attending to work, family, hobbies, and academic pursuits. Or perhaps you don't have the means to do those things so your time is spent in worry and survival mode about the future. Either way, it's easy for self-care to take a back seat to the many concerns of our lives. In this chapter we'll look at some basic building blocks of body nurture beginning with thought patterns and their physiological effect. We'll explore epigenetics—the study of how environmental factors influence our genetic expression—and our body's ability to prevent or succumb to genetic destiny. You'll get a clearer picture of the immense healing that takes place during your sleep cycles, and the value of your diet to the health and well-being of your mind. Lastly, we'll contemplate what it means to grow old with grace. These are all an integral part of neurosculpting, as each component has the power to support our gifts of neuroplasticity and our ability to change our predisposition to the world.

WHAT HAPPENS WHEN
WE DON'T NURTURE OURSELVES?

As we explored in the previous chapter, care and nourishment of our body-world has the potential to support the healing of our mental states. What if each smell, touch, sight, taste, and interaction were one of intentional nurturing? What if we could rely less on external caregivers whom we turn to when something is wrong and more on our own internal caregiver ability to perpetuate and enrich all that is right? The subtle messages the body gets from the environment through the senses communicate important messages to the brain. Think about those times when the hair on the back of your neck stood up. Or when you noticed your loved one's face angry and scowling. What messages do those sensory experiences signal to your brain? Do they evoke stories you use to interpret the nature of what's going on? We can rebuild ourselves from the inside out. But first we have to notice what's going on internally so we can begin to neurosculpt that dynamic.

Maybe you recall the discovery journal exercise from the previous chapter in which you identified areas of your body that typically get activated when you're feeling stress. These patterned responses are great examples of your body's sympathetic nervous system response. Your sympathetic nervous system is designed to create an arousal response, meaning when it's activated you are primed for mobilization, or fight-or-flight. Like any balanced system we come equipped with a parasympathetic relaxation response, which is designed to regulate, restore, repair, and recalibrate from our readiness response. When we experience stress (whether it be an oncoming car collision or the stress of work), our limbic system engages the sympathetic response, which we know to be a fight/flee/freeze response. In this case, the limbic system signals the release of our mobilization chemicals such as adrenaline and cortisol.

These hormones are fabulous in an emergency if we plan on using them to run, fight, or flee. But are you literally running from or fighting that worrisome thought you just brought up in your mind? Do you really need to freeze from the stress of work—is this really the most helpful response? This is an example of a perceived stress in which there's no real context for an in-the-moment physiological reaction. So if we trigger mobilization hormones but don't actually mobilize (fight or flee), we won't use those hormones for what they're designed for, or dissipate them. And if they're not used for their intended purpose, they begin to use *us*. Our sympathetic arousal in response to threat doesn't do us any good when there's no real survival risk at stake. How often do you trigger your own limbic response with a thought and then spend hours fighting phantoms? What process do you have in place to find compassion and care for yourself when you're in the grip of worrisome reactions to the world around you?

Here's what we're doing to ourselves when stress hormones like adrenaline kick up: We are recruiting blood flow from our internal organs and systems and sending it to the muscles and limbs for quick use, energy, mobility, strength, speed, increased sense of smell and hearing, and increased peripheral vision.[1] The heart rate increases to quickly pump oxygenated blood to the muscles, and the breath becomes more rapid and shallow. When blood is redirected like this, we then slow down the internal processes like digestion, absorption of nutrients, and the robust production of our immune system.

It makes perfect sense when you think about it. If you were an animal in the wild, eating your food, and suddenly you were attacked, you'd want all of your metabolic resources available for running. In order to do that, you'd stop digesting so that you could recruit all the potential energy in your body to your large muscles. This is why you might have noticed a dry throat during your stress thought, or contracted and tense muscles, or even a rapid heart rate or shallow breathing. You were bearing witness to the miraculous, instantaneous effect of adrenaline.

Over time, this is a dangerous cycle if it's overused. It can compromise our ability to absorb our nutrients, lessen our immunity, skew our ability to regulate our blood sugar, cause inflammation in the brain and joints, cause high blood pressure, and contribute to strokes, Type II diabetes, fibromyalgia, depression, substance abuse, foggy brain, multiple sclerosis, Parkinson's, and Alzheimer's—just to name a few. And here's something that science has discovered: the chronic elevation of cortisol in the body damages the hippocampus, which is in the center of the limbic system and is highly involved in creating and storing new memories *and* turning down the fight-or-flight response.[2] Through excessive stress, we actually damage the body's "off" switch for the stress process.

Imagine you have a terrible migraine and the bright lights in the room make it worse. You want to turn them off, but instead of flipping the switch, you are so angry that you throw a sledgehammer and crush the switch instead—with it stuck in the "on" position. Now you have painful lights adding to your migraine and no ability to shut them off. This is what the stress cycle can do to us. We begin feeling depleted and beaten up, like the version of myself I met in the Readyverse.

As we use and reuse neural networks, they become more efficient, and as we stop using them in a synchronized way, they prune themselves back. What we now know is that the gray matter of our brain grows! The more we use it, the denser it gets with dendrites and activity. So if you keep exercising those stress-based thoughts, you eventually broaden the neurological reach of the maps associated with those thoughts. And, if you don't actively practice positive thoughts the gray matter dedicated to those thoughts shrinks. If we were to use a metaphor and say that our gray matter is like a muscle, then which muscle do you want to continue to exercise and which do you really want to atrophy?

Take this metaphor further: Let's say our limbic fear-based threat response is represented by our right arm, which reaches out to the world with a fist in a defensive position. Our compassionate, empathetic PFC (prefrontal cortex) response is represented by our left arm, which reaches out to the world with an open handshake. Now, what if I tied your left arm behind your back for a year? First, your left-arm muscles will undoubtedly shrink. When I untie it, whether someone comes at you with anger or reaches out to you in generosity, you will only have your right arm and fist to meet that. You will have to work to rehabilitate the left arm, diligently, every day, in order to strengthen it back to balancing out the right arm. Then when someone comes at you with generosity, you will extend the open hand to shake, and when someone comes at you in threat, you can meet that with the fist. Without the exercise and commitment, you'll always default to the stronger muscle and become limited in your choices. As we engage consciously in neurosculpting we take charge of which part of the brain we exercise.

As a result of your stress response's insidious feedback loop, through what lens do you think you're going to see the world? Are you going to see the glass half empty or half full at that point? How easy will it be for you to find the silver lining? How well will you be there for those around you in need? How open will you be to seeing another's perspective? How much will you have left to give? You already know your answers.

· · · · · · · · · · · · ·

DISCOVERY JOURNAL identifying negative intent

For the next week, note in your journal all the times throughout the day in which you assumed negative intent when someone approached you or asked you a question. These are moments when you are defaulting to a patterned negative thought or response (which, thankfully, you can use neurosculpting to combat). Examples might be your response when your phone rings and you recognize a familiar phone number, yet you hesitate to answer it because you assume it will be an annoying conversation. Or maybe it's when your co-worker approaches you with a stack of papers in hand, and you immediately think it means more work. If there are times you can't identify any negative assumptions, then simply give yourself a star.

This exercise can help you begin to identify how steeped you are in a negative world lens. You can begin to notice if you are reaching out to others with an open and compassionate hand or if you're meeting all approaches with a closed-fist mentality.

So how can we move from a negative outlook into a real feeling of loving ourselves from the inside out and the outside in? Our inner negativity not ony affects our moods and behaviors, it also affects each of us at a cellular level. We can't hope to change anything about our world until we work on our inner stories first.

EPIGENETICS AND THE MAGIC FAMILY TREE

There are more studies than ever on the health benefits of meditation. We know that for centuries meditation has been used to calm the mind, find inner peace, and create states of acceptance and compassion. These practices have informed religions, institutions, and cultural expressions. We've moved from the belief and faith in meditative power to the science of meditation as we've begun to correlate meditation to lower heart rate, anger and pain management, and even as a supplement to some psychological therapies. We've begun to realize that meditation isn't only for clearing the mind and creating calm, but also has the power to alter our genetic blueprint—our DNA.

In one study published in the Public Library of Science, researchers measured changes in meditators' energy metabolism, mitochondrial function, insulin secretion, and telomere maintenance. Telomeres are our DNA indicator for healthful aging.[3] They are the beginning and end points of a gene, and they are linked to reduced inflammatory response and stress-related pathways. This means that our chosen and cultivated frame of mind has now been shown to increase the length of the beginning and end points of our genes. This is an example of the idea of epigenetics, which says that our genetic expression—once thought to be our fixed destiny based on our inherited traits—is not fixed at all. This is what I was doing to my spirit-self in my vision. I was clearing my mind and preparing it for compassion and self-nurturing so that I could rebuild myself beginning with my very own set of genetic instructions.

Environmental factors, how well we've been nurtured, and individual disposition all play a huge role in our genetic expression. Our DNA is no longer thought of as the conductor of our physical destiny, but more like an orchestra of all available instruments, which may be played or can remain silent.[4] It turns out that the conductor is actually you, and more particularly you *in relationship* to your inner and outer worlds.

In 2004, researchers at McGill University in Canada showed that the environment a rat pup grew up in could either turn on or off the gene for anxiety—regardless of whether or not the rat inherited the gene.[5]

Researchers identified rats with anxiety that had a heritable genetic code for that trait. That means that this trait would be passed on to the pups. Likewise, pups born to rats that did not have the anxiety trait would not pass anxiety on to their pups. After seeing these two groups of rats have babies that genetically matched the parental genetics, researchers noticed that there was a huge difference in the way the mother rats cared for their pups. Mother rats with the inheritable anxiety gene licked their pups less often than mother rats without the inheritable anxiety gene. So, licking became an environmental factor that researchers decided to look at.

Next, brand-new pups from each group were swapped in this experiment. Pups who had the anxiety gene were taken immediately after birth and given to a foster rat mother who had no anxiety gene, and vice versa. What happened was miraculous. Pups with the anxiety gene who were frequently licked actually turned off the expression of the anxiety gene at the DNA strand. And the pups that never inherited a genetic expression for anxiety actually activated one because they were not licked.

By licking, a mother rat can transmit and code genetic information via proteins directly onto the strand of DNA, which completely circumvents the process of genetic inheritance that happens during egg-sperm fertilization. This is the power of epigenetics, where a larger body of information from the environment affects the expressions of our genes on the DNA strand. These changes then become heritable traits in further offspring. What could this imply for each interaction we have with our children and parents? How does each gesture and word we say spin our cells like gears in a larger machine? How do our environments—inner and outer—turn our genes on or off for stress and anxiety? What kinds of environments can we create for ourselves so that we can lower our stress response in our daily lives?

I'm sure you've heard yourself say things like, "High blood pressure runs in my family" or "All the women in my family developed diabetes, so I probably will." And although inheritance is a huge part of our genetic makeup, it's not the whole picture. I think sometimes we give up our power and our seat as master of our own destiny when we default to a view that our physical destiny is only as healthy and whole as those who came before us. Epigenetics shows us that what we put in and on our bodies, who and what we choose to surround ourselves with, our hobbies, and even our mood, all contribute to the expression of the vast numbers of genes of our DNA code.

Epigenetics also means that our current experience can change the heritable traits of our DNA. There are some amazing insights into this process coming out of many laboratories around the world. In the Laboratory for Molecular Reproduction and Genetics at the Indian Institute of Medical Sciences in New Delhi, it has been discovered that the non-genetic changes that happen to sperm cells during the lifetime of the male will actually affect the healthy development of the fetus the sperm helps create.[6] This means that it's not *just* the father's genes that pass on to the baby, but also the changes and modifications made to those genes during the father's lifetime based on his lifestyle, health, and nutritional choices. These modifications then get passed along with the original gene to the offspring. We are living in a time when entire laboratories of scientists note that "Various lifestyle modifications (such as the increased intake of fruits and vegetables, exercise, *meditation*, yoga, cessation of smoking, and reduction in alcohol intake) can improve the health of the sperm genome and result in normal embryonic development and the birth of healthy offspring [italics added]."[7]

This implies drastic consequences for our children due to an unconscious approach to our own lives in the present moment. How might you look at your choices differently knowing that each decision can have a ripple effect far into the future?

Since the thoughts we think consciously and unconsciously have the power to engage our stress hormones, which affect the environment of the blood and cells, then our thoughts have epigenetic influence on our cells as well. Every nucleus in our cells exists inside a larger environment, and each cell exists inside yet a larger environment of tissue, blood, or bone. Epigenetics explains how the changes in the environment affect what the DNA in the nucleus will express. So how does the DNA get information about the changes in the environment? Protein messengers are like tiny little informants that travel between the nucleus and the cell membrane to collect data about what's going on "out there."[8] They communicate that data back to the nucleus and the DNA. When we are engaged in stressful and negative thoughts about ourselves, others, or the world around us, the hormones we release will end up chemically changing the environment of the cell. If "out there" is a large pool of stress hormones, like adrenaline and cortisol, or excessive inflammation from stress or disease, then the proteins communicate a very different message about the environment to the DNA than they would if the body was regulated and in a state of calm, joy, and compassion. Will the message be that the world "out there" is hostile? Our DNA will be less likely to transcribe, activate, silence, and translocate genetic code correctly in a hostile environment. And this is precisely how disease can be created or perpetuated. So what we think and how well we learn how to bring ourselves back to restoration and relaxation has an influence on how genes in our DNA activate.

When we create a mental entrainment or meditation practice that takes charge of our negative stories, we can support a healthy cellular environment. We have more control over our body's toxic environment than maybe we initially thought. We already know that our fear-based and negative thought patterns initiate and perpetuate a cascade of stress reactions, and the converse is also true. In other words, our stress reactions increase the likelihood that we will have fear-based and negative thought patterns. We *know* that we reduce adrenaline and cortisol levels with meditation. We *know* meditation increases our immunity. We *know* meditation helps regulate blood sugar and metabolism. Therefore, we *know* we have a direct impact on our genetic destiny right here, right now, in each and every moment. If we don't take responsibility for our thoughts, then we burden ourselves, our loved ones, and even strangers with the future weight of our unhealthy minds and bodies. Because meditation is a cornerstone of the neurosculpting process, we are in a constant state of renegotiating our stress response. Whether it's breathing exercises, entrainment practices, or a meditative journey that you'll read about later in this book, your commitment to a regular practice is in direct support of the best possible version of you.

• • • • • • • • • • • •

DISCOVERY JOURNAL **commitment to change**

Note three easy lifestyle changes you can make beginning this week that you'll maintain for at least one month. Examples might be to reduce your intake of soda, add at least one more vegetable to your dinner plate, or spend ten extra minutes a week in cultivating positive thoughts or in a neurosculpting practice. As you follow through on your commitments, at the end of the month add in three more easy lifestyle changes you can make. Continue this process.

GETTING A GOOD NIGHT'S SLEEP—
MORE THAN JUST A RECOMMENDATION

Many of us have heard since we were young that getting a good night's sleep is important to our health and well-being. And because we sleep every night, and have since birth, it's very easy to take this vital process for granted, not really understanding how this is critical for our ability to cultivate care and nourishment for ourselves. While scientists continue to study the function of sleep, we already know that it's vital for a sharp mind and positive mood. Current research suggests that sleep, particularly when we dream, is an important biological process of long-term memory consolidation. Memory consolidation is a time when the brain strengthens the mental traces of an event by integrating new elements with older versions and other stored information. This process helps us maintain the stability of our memories as we proceed into new and uncharted territory each day.[9] Having a healthy method of memory consolidation and a safe place like dreams in which to rehearse complex emotional states seems critical in our ability to exercise our memory centers and continually adapt and update them with new integrated information. Dreams can be viewed as a neurosculpting sandbox in which we modify our old stories to keep ourselves present. I wonder if I'd ever have understood that I needed to take better care of the neglected self I met in my vision had I not had my own dreams.

More than having an opportunity to sculpt our thoughts and memories, sleep is a survival mechanism. Prolonged sleep deprivation can actually be fatal. How much sleep is a healthy amount for you? Each of us will answer that differently depending on our body and our lifestyle. Generally speaking, the older we get, the less sleep we need in order to maintain a healthy mind and body. In utero we are sleeping almost all of the time. As an infant in our first year we probably slept about sixteen hours a day with that number decreasing the older we got until full adulthood where most of us require somewhere between six and eight hours of regular sleep each twenty-four-hour cycle.

What's Happening When We Sleep?

When we sleep we engage in natural circadian rhythms, which usually occur every twenty-four hours. During these natural cycles our sleep time allows our nervous system a homeostatic regulation—it gets to normalize. During these times we're experiencing hormonal regulation, body temperature regulation, tissue repair, mental reprocessing, and restoration. We have a molecular clock in the brain that is entrained to the night and day cycles of our world through its connection to the retina in our eyes. In many ways our environment is guiding us to sleep at certain times. Battling against these natural environmental rhythms can result in compromised sleep and disregulated patterns.[10]

During sleep we are moving through different brain wave frequency cycles, some slower and some faster than others, where our electromagnetic output from the brain varies. All of these correspond to one of two distinct parts of our sleep patterns: non-REM sleep where we are slowing down our active mind and REM sleep where we are in a paradoxical state of dreaming that quiets the body and muscle response but activates a form of awake mind that can entertain thoughts and experiences. Delta waves, which are generally the slowest (1–4 Hz, or cycles per second), are indicative of our deepest moments of sleep. After Delta waves come Theta waves, which are a bit faster (4–7 Hz), and are generally associated with our waking state. Next come Alpha waves (7–14 Hz), which can be associated with those times in our waking state when our eyes are closed and we are tuning in to the environment with less sensory stimulation. Lastly, we have Beta waves (14–40 Hz) and Gamma waves (anything above 40 Hz), which can relate to our experiences of focused mental attention.

You probably know from your own experience that once you've disregulated your hormones, waking cycles, and sleep it's far easier to succumb to normal stress, and perhaps even perceive excessive stress where you might not have before. Remember, cortisol elevates during your stress response and can damage the hippocampus, which is precisely what we need to have healthy in order to continue to access our memories, integrate new information, and create new learning. Lack of adequate sleep can have a negative domino effect on our ability to write our stories in an ever-adaptive process of emotional, mental, and spiritual evolution.

We have five stages of sleep in a normal sleep cycle:

STAGE 1   We get drowsy and our waking brain wave patterns are beginning to synchronize across different areas of the brain.

STAGE 2   We fall into a deeper sleep where we are experiencing short bursts of electrical synchrony. This stage might pass after about fifteen or twenty minutes of sleep.

STAGE 3   We now experience even more slowing down of brain waves.

STAGE 4   We are in the deepest level of sleep, where the brain is in the slow Delta brain wave pattern. We might be in this pattern between one and one-and-a-half hours.

STAGE 5   We are in REM sleep, which means rapid eye movement. This part of the sleep cycle resembles brain waves we have when we are getting drowsy at the onset of our sleep cycle. This cycle is paradoxical in that it's like being awake while we sleep.

Sleep Deprivation's Assassination of the Self-Nurturer

Sleep deprivation affects both body and mind, and can have a profound effect on our day-to-day functioning. Not only is it more difficult to concentrate, it's harder to maintain a healthy body state. Within just days of sleep deprivation we may experience weight gain and an inability to function well off a normal caloric intake.[11] It's also been shown that sleep deprivation is directly linked to mood disregulation and even increased risk of suicidal behavior in teenagers.[12] With such a correlation between normal sleep cycles and positive mental and emotional health, how can we expect to be our best self, caring for ourselves with compassion and for others, if we are not engaging in one of our fundamental mechanisms for positive plasticity? The journey through healing trauma, rewriting our beliefs, and finding wholeness requires our sleep foundation be solid, consistent, and deep.

• • • • • • • • • • • •

DISCOVERY JOURNAL   a foundation built from awareness

This exercise is a bit more long term. Be prepared to keep your journal by your bedside for the next week. In your journal make four columns titled: "Bedtime," "Fell Asleep," "Awoke Prematurely," and "Wake Up Time." Each night before bed note the time you settle in for the evening. This may not be the time you fall asleep. Most of us don't fall asleep right away. If you happen to be one of the people who glances at the clock before falling off to sleep you may be able to note the approximate time you fell asleep in that column *in the morning.* Don't interrupt your drowsiness to record that. If you are one of those individuals who wakes periodically throughout the night you can also note that in the morning in your journal column called "Premature Waking." Finally, note the time you wake up. After a week notice your average sleep cycles. If you are not getting a deep and regular sleep you may be able to identify patterns of when you're waking up or how long it's taking you to fall asleep. It's easy to dismiss a challenged night of sleep as something that just happens from time to time. In this dismissal we may miss that it's an actual pattern. This exercise will help you identify if you are in a disregulated sleep pattern, or if a night of challenged sleep is truly just a unique occurrence. If you notice a pattern you now have a platform from which to investigate behaviors and methods to help you regulate again. Some examples of practices you could put in place might be:

- Darken the bedroom at night with heavier shades or an eye mask.
- Stay off computers or mind-active stimulation for longer periods of time before bed to help the mind slow down.
- Don't eat foods before bed that would spike your blood sugar, such as carbohydrates.
- As much as possible, sleep at night and be awake during the day.

WHAT DOES FOOD HAVE TO DO WITH A SHARP MIND?

Sleep is not the only foundation you can adapt in order to help you be your best self. What and how we feed our bodies directly supports how we feed our mind and spirit. Imagine how poorly your brand new luxury car would run if it required regular fuel but you filled it up with diesel. Many of us are more conscious about what we put in our expensive cars than in our own body. Eating a well-balanced diet of carbohydrates, fats, and proteins is vital not just to physical health, but it's critical to mental health as well. We need to consume carbohydrates so we have sugar to convert into the body's fuel. We need to consume fats for the proper care of our cell membranes, the building blocks of our brain matter, and the conductive quality of our axons, which carry signals sent from our neurons. We need to eat protein to build structures like muscles, blood, bones, and neurotransmitters. The three of these together give us the necessary foundations for a healthy and vibrant life. When we consume an imbalance of these, we become imbalanced in our body and mind.

Think about this carefully. Lack of healthy protein in favor of an excess of carbohydrates means we'd lack the essential amino acids necessary to form our neurotransmitters. Our neurotransmitters—like dopamine, serotonin, oxytocin, gaba, acetylcholine, and more—are all intricately involved in the orchestration of our moods, focus, perceptions, dispositions, motivations, ability to learn, desire to mate, and on and on. If you don't consume enough healthy fats, then you would further compromise the ability of your already-compromised neurotransmitters to signal proper communication in the brain. Ask yourself, how long do you think you'd sustain a positive outlook and mental sharpness if your diet doesn't support the building blocks of positivity and cognitive agility?

The relationship of food to our mental and physical health goes even deeper. If you compromise your ability to regulate mood, then it's easy to slip into a fear-based or fight-or-flight disposition. This stress state, and its associated hormonal increase in adrenaline and cortisol, begins to cause chronic problems with the way in which we convert sugar to fuel. In this compromised state, our cells produce far too many free radicals as a by-product of this labored conversion. Free radicals are the oxidized molecules that form as we convert sugar to storable fuel. These molecules are like the exhaust fumes of a car. The cleaner the exhaust, the better for the environment. Too many free radicals harm the body's environment. This results in inflammation. A chronic cycle like this has the ability to inhibit our body's natural power to keep certain unhealthy genes turned off. Once we remove our ability to keep destructive genes in an off position, we risk turning them on and having a proliferation of unhealthy genes replicating and translocating themselves—and sometimes this is called cancer!

So if we could supply the right balance of building blocks for all of our body's needs, we could create a rich mind-body platform that enables us to feel more in control of our moods and genetic destiny. So why wouldn't you want to be a little more conscious of that mix?

I love our nutritional therapist's motto at the Neurosculpting Institute. She says that her one strict rule is "everything on a plate." If you put all of your food on a plate and sit at a table with your feet on the floor, you will be in a much different space when eating that food. You will have established a relationship with it in preparing it. With all of your food on a plate, you'll be able to see whether the basic food groups are represented. This gives you an opportunity to modify it if you need to. By sitting at a table, we force ourselves to slow down. As a society used to eating on the go, we compromise our body's ability to absorb nutrients when we are using resources to fuel our "go" mode while we're trying to fuel our digestion.

In striving for a healthy balance of carbohydrates, proteins, and fats, it's handy to know what goes into these food groups. The best forms of carbohydrates to consume are vegetables and fruits. We've heard a lot about the perils of refined carbohydrates and certain grains, but many of us think if we stay away from bread, then we've tackled the carbohydrate issue. This is not true. Bread is just one of the many types of carbohydrates we consume.

In fact, I know plenty of very health-conscious people who think their breakfast of fruit, granola, and juice is a healthy way to start the day. The reality is that that sort of meal is a breakfast of only carbohydrates, and it is far from balanced. That is like injecting sugar directly into your veins. You'll be spiking your blood sugar, feeding your reactionary fight-or-flight cycle, and setting yourself up for a nice crash sometime mid-morning. Over time, this kind of carbohydrate-heavy lifestyle will cause your body to overproduce insulin, cortisol, and free radicals, create more inflammation, cause disturbed sleep cycles, cause weight gain, and favor a limbic stress- and fear-based disposition to the world.

There's more and more research coming out about how detrimental sugar and carbohydrates are to our cognitive functioning. Thankfully, we have leaders in the medical field who are willing to give the general public this information and help overturn the idea that breads, grains, and carbohydrates belong in the largest group on our food plate. Our own medical science journals now show evidence that a diet high in fats and low in carbohydrates and sugar actually reduces a person's body fat, triglycerides, blood sugar, and blood pressure, and increases their HDL cholesterol.[13]

In such a body environment, the brain's prefrontal cortex has enough of its own main building block: fat. Having enough healthy fat in our diet helps replace and replenish the main supporting component of our brain, which is about 60 percent fat by weight. If we starve the brain of fat, then our brain becomes malnourished, exhausted, and begins to function poorly. Our neurons are no longer able to send signals efficiently, as their axons conduct the signal when their myelin sheath is fortified with fat.

Once this happens, it's far easier for the limbic system to take over—even more than it already does. We are eating our way into a stressful lifestyle that primes us, not so gracefully, to exhibit many of our most insidious neurodegenerative diseases, some of which include depression and suicide. We're also seeing research that shows there's an inverse relationship between a person's level of blood sugar and the size of their hippocampus, which is known as the memory center of the limbic system. Those who have higher levels of blood sugar show shrinkage in this area of the brain.[14]

I grew up on pasta and fondly remember drinking Coca-Cola with dinner almost every night. I started my mornings with two to three glasses of orange juice and oatmeal, ate a sandwich for lunch, and pasta with bread for dinner. In fact, my all-time favorite meal growing up was a most delicious Sicilian tradition in our house: pasta with fried breadcrumbs and Italian bread! Yes, my mouth waters to think about it while my brain recoils in horror. Talk about cognitive dissonance! We'd fry up seasoned breadcrumbs and sprinkle them on top of our pasta like a condiment. Then we'd reach for a chunk of bread from the basket on the table and use that to help scoop up the pasta. It was a decadent, incestuous carbohydrate orgy—and none of us knew what profound damage it could do. If my fuel consistently starved my brain of some key building blocks like fat and protein, and my limbic system gained dominance because it knew how to function on a compromised diet, then how likely do you think it would be that my inner thoughts would be positive, compassionate, and graceful? Not very.

If you take the time to put your food on your plate, you might realize you are missing protein and fat in that meal. And if you modify each meal to strive toward a more tasty balance, you could be giving your body some substantial support as you try to regulate your stress, grow your health, and connect to the compassionate parts of yourself that seem to get beaten down when you are sick and malnourished. Remember, what and how we feed our bodies directly supports how we feed our mind and spirit.

The body's fuel doesn't feed just the body; it feeds the potential that we can reach our highest human expression. It feeds the very interface the soul has chosen through which to express its divine mission.

Antioxidants are a huge key in supporting our mind's healthy ability to stay sharp, adaptable, and young. Antioxidants are molecules present in some of the food we eat. Their important job is to help quench the excessive number of free radicals that flood our bodies from our own cells. Consider a brand new bicycle left out all winter in the rain and snow. In the spring you'd find the smooth metal to be rusted, brittle, and cracking. This is an example of the oxidation process. Our cells experience the same thing. We naturally produce oxidized molecules which, left unattended, will cause a chain reaction inside our cells and eventually damage the cell and its membrane. Our best defense against this is to consume foods that stop this process from spiraling out of control. We need to *anti*-oxidize. Eating foods rich in antioxidants is like parking the bicycle in a dry garage all winter long.

We produce more free radicals if the environment of the cell is compromised by stress. This is a critical link in our long-term health. The more we manage our free radicals, the more we regulate inflammation, cell life, energy use—our life force. Managing this process can directly support a sharp mind, a reduced inflammatory stress response, and access to a more vital life. Ask yourself if it's easier for you to be your best self when you're sick and weak or when you're vibrant and strong.

As you are taking the balance of your food into consideration, you could make a list of easily accessible antioxidant foods you like and try to add them to your meals. Some examples of antioxidant-rich foods include:

- Blueberries, blackberries, raspberries, strawberries, and cranberries
- Red beans
- Pecans
- Artichokes, cabbage, broccoli, and garlic
- Red wine
- Green and black teas
- Unsweetened and dark chocolate

• • • • • • • • • • • •

what are you putting in your body?

A great way to start noticing your food is to keep a basic journal of what you eat for a week. Note everything you have for breakfast, snacks, lunch, and dinner for at least five to seven days. At the end of each day, see if you can notice whether your intake was balanced between fats, proteins, and carbohydrates, or whether perhaps you were lacking one entire food category. You can try adding some food items from the antioxidant list to your meals starting with one item per day.

Relationship to Our Food Sources

What if we knew exactly where our food came from, what went into the life cycle of that meal, and all the hands involved in getting that food to our plate? How would we eat differently if we had an in-depth relationship to the food we consumed? I must admit that for many years, I was a very unconscious eater, reaching for what was convenient and tasted good. I didn't have many rules or even ethics around my food, and I always marveled at those who did. My best friend had been a vegetarian since we were young, and I always respected her commitment to a cause, even if I didn't share that commitment. She seemed to be conscious about what she put in her body, and I did not care all that much about what went into mine.

My profound understanding of what a real relationship with food is was changed by a third-person story I heard from a survivalist when I was studying primitive survival skills. A little boy, whose father was a skilled hunter, dearly loved his winter mukluks. As he grew out of these warm winter boots and the next winter approached, he asked his father to make him another pair. His father agreed, but not without the boy's participation in the boot-making process. The boy was excited to go with his father to get the materials at a friend's farm. As the pair drove up in their truck to the farm, the boy was horrified to see a cow hanging upside down, partially butchered. The father told the boy to get out of the car, but he was terrified and began to cry. He asked why they were hurting the cow. The father, now losing his patience, asked the boy if he knew that his favorite food—hamburgers—didn't just come from frozen packages in the grocery store, but from actual living animals. The boy was shocked. The father told him that until he had a relationship to his food sources, he had no business eating that food or wearing those boots.

This story changed the way I saw food. My body, my soul's temple, was feeding and fueling off a source of food from which I was completely disconnected. If thoughts matter to our physicality, then what would happen if I began to cultivate a relationship of reverence and gratitude for the food I ate, whether I was a carnivore, vegetarian, or vegan? If you had a reverence for the food you consumed, would you waste any? Would you consume gratuitously? Would you begin to choose different foods that meant something more to you?

Eating in a state of unconsciousness, on the go, rushed or even stressed out, all compromise our ability to absorb the nutrients we need. Remember, when we are in a state of sympathetic arousal we have elevated stress hormones whose job it is to divert blood away from the internal organs and toward the large muscle masses. If this happens while we are eating, then we actually slow digestion and impair the gut's ability to do its job while we starve it of its vital fuel. Having a negative or unconscious relationship to the fuel we put in our bodies can directly affect how we use that fuel.

Here's an interesting ritual I began doing before each meal to establish a relationship with my food. I looked at each item on my plate and imagined that plant's or animal's full life cycle, including the food and resources it needed to live as well. I then imagined all of the people it took to take that one piece of food from its life to my plate, including processing and transportation. This only takes a few seconds, but by the time you finish you might realize the massive amount of time, energy, resources, and people involved in one simple meal. The more you create this sort of relationship with your food, the more you will savor each bite and be appreciative of all the abundance and fortune that created that full plate. It's difficult to be wasteful, stressed, or greedy when we start recognizing these relationships. Additionally, this simple ritual focuses our awareness and activates the PFC by forcing us to consider others—both of which bring us out of a stress response prior to eating. Reverence is a natural result.

Neurosculpting around food means changing our thought patterns to be in a dynamic and real-time relationship with all that we eat, rather than in an unconscious pattern. Each moment we nourish our bodies is a moment we can use our thoughts to enhance that nourishment. If we separate mind, body, and spirit, then the food we put in our bodies would have little to do with the mind and spirit. Would we still be able to be our highest and best self while living on junk food? Of course, this is simply not the case.

The fuel we digest matters a great deal to the way the brain functions and to whether or not it defaults to stress; it matters to our brain's ability to be empathetic and compassionate; and it matters to our spirit to have a body that can do good works in the world. When we are not in a positive relationship to our food, then we impair our body's ability to use that fuel productively. A healthy body is a crucial component of a healthy mind and spirit, as we're learning they are all parts of the greater whole.

With an increased awareness of how to positively influence our genetics, how to ensure our plasticity and memory consolidation with regulated sleep cycles, and what to eat to help support a more fluid dynamic between our prefrontal cortex and limbic system, consider this question: If you do all of this will you age more consciously?

ARE YOU READY FOR THE RETIREMENT HOME?

Aging gracefully is something I think we all can put on our wish list. I doubt any of us wants to age quickly into states of physical debilitation or cognitive impairment. Yet many of the images and experiences we have with the elderly tell a different story. I think many of us have this question in the backs of our minds: "Who will care for me when I'm old?"—or perhaps we've even resolved ourselves to the vision that inevitably we must end up in an elderly care center because we are too ill to care for ourselves. It's amazing how this vision has become a fairly accepted collective conscious image of our twilight years.

To demonstrate the power of story, I want to share one that I heard about the renowned survivalist Tom Brown Jr. and his Apache "grandfather." One of Tom's students shared this with me when I attended Tom's survival school.

Tom was taught by Stalking Wolf, an Apache elder, from age eight to eighteen. He was taught the survival, tracking, and medicine ways of the scout. By the time he was done with his studies he was able to track a mouse trail across a gravel expanse the size of a football field. He could look at the tracks of animals, invisible to most eyes, and know if the animal had a full or empty belly, if it had a voided or full bladder, if it was pregnant, and ultimately where it could be found. If you were to meet him, you'd truly believe in super powers, and the tales say that even he isn't as skilled as his Apache grandfather was.

About the time Tom was turning eighteen, his grandfather, who by then was very old—some say around ninety—went on regular scout missions with him. This meant that Tom was to track Grandfather through the Pine Barrens, reading the leaves, trees, tracks, and trails in order to find him.

At a certain point Tom came across Grandfather's medicine bag, left intentionally in sight. To us this might not mean anything. To Tom this was a life-changing event. It meant that Grandfather had gone off to die, and that he was leaving his legacy for Tom to pick up. This image of Grandfather in this story is *not* the image of the frail man in the nursing home who's been wired up with tubes and IVs. This is the image of a man completely in command of his destiny.

Imagine being healthy enough in both mind and body well into your nineties to recognize when it was your time to go, and then doing so on your own terms. Imagine being independent and productive all the minutes of your life until the last. Imagine unsubscribing to the mental and physical health image many of us buy into.

I visited my grandmother often when she could no longer care for herself. She was treated well, mostly because my mother and aunts spent every day in the retirement home making their presence known and advocating for those who had no one to fight for them. Still, it was not the most positive environment. Privacy and autonomy did not exist, and "residents" were housed in glorified hospital rooms. It felt to me like a place people went to die slowly rather than to thrive and get the most out of their precious time. And as far as homes go, she had a good one. I can only imagine how toxic the bad ones must be.

This is what so many of us project in our mind's eye when we think of our own aging. Does this description make you want to race to your own finish line, eager to reach these last few years? Hardly! Built in to our collective picture of aging is a resistance and fear response, so that by the time we get there, we've already spent years cultivating negativity around it. So how do we undo the collective momentum defining our twilight years?

Keeping ourselves healthy, although different for each of our needs and lifestyles, still involves a few basic things that we all know and have heard before. Twenty minutes of enjoyable cardio exercise a day not only works the muscles but also has been shown to stimulate brain-derived neurotrophic factor (BDNF), which is a growth hormone in the brain that helps the hippocampus birth brand new neurons.[15] New neurons mean new cognitive potential. Imagine staying mentally sharp our entire lives! Why not start this regimen right now? Consider these activities as regular additions to your week:

- Four brisk walks in your favorite neighborhood for twenty minutes each time.
- Five minutes of daily stretching in the morning and ten minutes of daily stretching in the evening.
- Take the stairs whenever possible.
- Get up from your desk at least once an hour and walk somewhere.

A LOOK BACK AT YOUR SPIRIT SELF

If you could look at your ether self in a mirror, or visit with it like I did in my vision, would you see a radiant image of vibrant health because of all the self-nurturing you've done throughout your life? Perhaps the image smiles back, or maybe it's shredded, neglected, and forlorn like mine was. You've been armed with the key building blocks of self-care in this chapter: thought rewiring, sleep support, exercise, and food. What do you think the image of your spirit self will look like a year from now after you've begun to cultivate an embodied nurtured state of being? How do you think consciously caring for yourself can support your sense of self-confidence? How empowered do you think you'll be as you shape yourself into old age with a conscious attention to self-care?

* * * * * * * * * * * * * * *

PUTTING IT ALL TOGETHER **cultivating self-care**

An important way to entrain the logistical information in this chapter is to look back at each section and note any commitments or important take-away ideas in the margins.

Epigenetics Section

As you review this section you might note specific ways in which you intend to manage your stress and your thoughts this week. Put your exercise on your calendar, and reminders to yourself to take the stairs when possible.

Sleep Section

Review this section and note the specific changes you are making to enhance or support your regular sleep cycles. Circle suggestions from the list you plan on implementing and put a date next to each one noting when you will implement that suggestion. Ask yourself these questions:

• How content and confident do you feel about yourself after a few nights of restless sleep?

- How content and confident do you feel about yourself after a few nights of deep sleep?

Food Section

Scan this section and highlight any foods from the food list that you will add to your diet to help balance your meals, or note extra ones in the margins. Take a look in your pantry and refrigerator and take note of the percentage of your total food that falls into the carbohydrate category. Try cutting your grain intake, and notice how you feel. Take a moment before your family meals to discuss how many different plants or animals helped contribute to your meal. You can also discuss how many steps and people you think were involved in processing the food to make it consumer-ready. Create a few words that will become your before-meal statement of gratitude. Find a family or friend food-buddy with whom you often eat to keep each other reminded of what a balanced meal looks like and move away from a grain-based diet. Start a compost pile and a small garden—even a potted garden—and participate in the growth cycle of some of your favorite vegetables.

5

the search for enough

When you are discontent, you always want more, more, more.
Your desire can never be satisfied. But when you practice
contentment, you can say to yourself, "Oh yes—
I already have everything that I really need."

His Holiness the 14th DALAI LAMA

I floated somewhere in a vast space between dreams and waking. I
was told to extract one tiny cell from the center of my heart, to pull it
out and hold it in front of me. It seemed so small, but it buzzed with
the life and mechanisms of galaxies. The Mother told me to pull out
one mitochondria and extract its ring-shaped DNA so I could look
only upon the ring. It was murky, dirty, and flaky like a rusty tube. I
noticed its brittle nature.

"This is not how it has to be," she said. So I began to clean it
off, peeling away the layers of brick-red crumbles until there was a
smooth and shiny ring. She asked me about the color and quality of
vitality. I somehow knew what that was: spring green and glowing
like neon. I was told to inject that color directly into the ring, allowing it to glow and radiate. It was easy, and the ring responded. Next,
she asked me to notice the color and quality of perfect health, then
strength, vibrance, and resilience. I did the same with each, injecting
a radiant spectrum into this ring until it was brighter than I could
stand. It pulsed all on its own, a blinding rainbow orb, and I knew

this was its highest natural state. It was ready to sink back into the mitochondria, settle into its new grandeur. As I put the mitochondria back into the cell like a gentle wave, this light spread to all the other mitochondria in the cell, vibrating each into unison. They hummed like well-oiled machines, singing a harmony with the fabric of the universe.

And then she went further, telling me to allow this light to communicate with my DNA. The double helix lit up, highlighting areas of open access and areas of great chromatin compaction. It didn't matter . . . light penetrated everywhere until the strand came hopefully alive with this rainbow contagion. Like bees in a hive, tiny components and proteins in my cell hurried about this strand with excitement . . . chattering messages of vibrance and healing. They transcribed genetic material in perfect elocution. I tasted a fluency of sound-light. My body sensed its own synesthetic nature.

My entire being warmed and yearned for the full enfolding of this cell. I placed this tiny orb of universal light back into my heart and watched a slow and deliberate expansion, a widespread influence systematically tuning my physical form to match this vibration. First my heart, then my lungs, until organ by organ I was vibrating a molecular synchrony. I felt complete and full, like the sun radiating with infinite potential. What worlds could I create from here?

I'M NOT GOOD ENOUGH

I questioned this vision many times, recalling the sense of feeling complete and full. I wondered often how to pull the amazing experience I had with The Mother into my day-to-day life so that I could find healing and wholeness. Clues to this process came through my amazing circle of friends. True friends can be great at offering support, wisdom, and companionship. I am blessed to have a wonderful group of friends who are not very interested in competition. No matter how much time passes, when we come together, it's usually supportive, empowering, and uplifting.

Some of the women in my group of friends have an ongoing tradition of meeting up for potlucks.

At these gatherings, we each take turns noting our high points and low points for the week or month. We don't try to solve each other's problems; we just create a space to voice these things. It was my friend's turn. She very casually told us her high point, then her voice became deeper and more sullen as she simply grumbled for her low, "Don't ever try jumping up and down naked in front of a full-length mirror." In a frozen moment where each one of us gazed off into a glazed-over distance this raw mini movie ran through each of our minds. Each of us gripped by the shock value of imagining our own selves naked and jumping.

Raucous laughter filled the room in commiseration. My first response was, "Don't worry, I will *never* do that!" And then a momentary realization woke me up: I wasn't even brave enough to do that because I knew what I'd see—my imperfect human-ness. How sad that so many of us have an aversion to seeing what's really there.

What insidious beliefs make it painful to look upon ourselves with acceptance? What levels of shame, comparison, or self-deprecation cause us to avoid our own natural reflections? Would I have reacted the same way if I had an innate sense that I was enough, as is? Think hard about these next questions and be honest with yourself. What would it take for you to sing that song on stage? Or to approach that one person you've always wanted to talk to? Or to speak up in that group of strangers? What would it take for you to be able to stand naked in front of a mirror and walk away feeling happier and more fulfilled than before you looked? Does that even seem like a reality? What messages are you sending about your own body-world when you look in the mirror?

Remember, if Dr. Ramachandran (chapter 3) could cure phantom limb syndrome by having his patients look in a mirror and neurologically respond to the illusion they saw, then what are we neurologically responding to when we don't like what we see each time we look at our own reflections?

. . . .

DISCOVERY JOURNAL
what do you need to feel like you are enough?

Answer these questions in your journal. Be as honest as you can with your own answers!

1 What do you need to see in the mirror in order to think highly of yourself?

2 How much of that do you already see each time you look in the mirror?

3 Can you stand completely naked in front of the mirror and remain loving, nonjudgmental, and happy in your self-talk?

4 What percentage of your body image do you feel you want to change? What percentage do you want to keep?

5 What activities or engagements cause you to have straight posture, where your shoulders are pulled back, your chin up, and your chest and stomach relaxed?

6 What activities or engagements cause you to slouch or go inward and try to become invisible?

7 What is the nature of your thoughts about your body after healthy food, pleasant and moderate physical activity, and stimulating hobbies? Do you focus as negatively on your image during these times?

8 What is the nature of your thoughts about your body after unhealthy food, mundane or imposed activity, and monotony? Do you focus more on your image during these times?

9   What anesthetizing substances do you consume when
    you are emotionally upset or feeling low self-esteem?
    Does it make you feel better? If so, for how long?

10 What is the nature of your thoughts when your body
    is sick or in physical pain?

11 Where are your typical areas of muscle tightness
    when you are stressed?

12 What sort of shift do you notice in your bowel
    regularity during stressful or emotional times?

These are ongoing questions that are designed to help you look at patterns of thoughts, self-esteem, and body physiology, which is why we took such a close look at self-care in the previous chapter. Once we begin caring for ourselves like our own prized possession, we can develop a deeper sense of value. When we feel our intrinsic value, then we can feel content and whole. The more I nurture myself the easier it is for me to place a higher value on myself. A pattern for me was always to say yes to everyone else and forget about myself. I'd inconvenience myself often to prioritize others' needs. I believed this was the way one showed compassion. And while this is one way to show others generosity and compassion, it came at my own expense. I'd find myself putting everyone else's needs before mine until eventually I was bitter, cynical, and resenting those times I answered the phone for a friend in need. This was not how I wanted to be. As I began caring for myself by taking the time to meditate, eat right, and check in with how I was feeling before committing to any course of action, the easier it was to be a genuinely giving person. There were times when I learned to say no if it meant the giving came from an empty place. My ability to be there for my friends got deeper because each giving came from a place of value and fullness. I had to cultivate and nurture my own self so that I could give more powerfully from a place of deep worth.

Perhaps you didn't even realize your food choices affected your self-esteem patterns. I notice that when I rely too much on carbohydrates for my daily fuel I don't feel as happy or vibrant. I become short with those I love and then begin to reprimand myself for my lack of patience. Maybe you are now seeing a relationship between your posture and when you feel comfortable with yourself. The intention is to get you comfortable viewing these concepts of self-care in relation to each other and not as isolated states of being. This becomes your platform of inquiry from which to build your sense of being enough. The more we understand our personal big picture, the more opportunity we have to create solutions we may not have seen before. My big picture was that I didn't have enough self-worth to give time and energy to myself the way I was giving it to others. This big picture caused me to identify the many ways in which I could begin caring for myself to finally feel like enough. As we change our relationship to ourselves, we begin sculpting our brain in a very different way. We no longer engage in our old stories of *not good enough* and those begin to lose their stronghold on our mental state.

THE SABOTEUR

As I cultivated more self-acceptance I began to realize that my inner saboteur, usually hard at work making things extra difficult, was, in fact, quieting down. What deep story activates your own sense of self-sabotage? Do you find yourself coming up with excuses just when you have opportunities presented to you that you've yearned for? Do you find yourself becoming extra clumsy before you're expected to perform something with grace? Do you make your worst decisions precisely at the times when good fortune requires you to be steadfast?

Why do we self-sabotage? Isn't it because precisely at the time when our luck could change for the better or things could finally go in our positive direction we somehow access a belief or script that says something like:

- This is too good to be true.
- I don't deserve this.
- I can't sustain this.

These statements come from a story that implies our sense of intrinsic self-worth does not match the circumstances, so therefore we must abandon ship. Think about all the times you've sabotaged yourself in that great relationship, or with that job, or in that circle of friends. Can you honestly say you would have chosen the same actions if you felt a sense of self-acceptance and wholeness? When we come to a place of feeling as though we're enough it's easy to not only sustain the choices and opportunities we create, but to attract even more.

Armed with the power of observation you will be equipped to make different decisions for yourself, and you will feel less pushed around by life's emotional ride. This empowerment correlates to an active pre-frontal cortex, which perceives an influence over life's circumstances. This is a move away from the self-deprecating victim and toward the person who simply "is enough" just as is. As we nurture ourselves we build our self-esteem, and as that grows we may find we have an abundance of self-love ready to be lavished upon our own lives, and then more freely on others.

SCULPTING YOURSELF

We live in such a high-stimulus world where images flash in front of us so quickly that we are bombarded by points of comparison in all moments. New gadgets, cars, careers, academic degrees, houses, and travel all become displayed in enticing ways from moment to moment as though we should have them, or strive to be like these images. We may find ourselves more frequently wondering things like *Do I have enough? Did I accomplish enough? Did I accomplish it fast enough? Did I present myself with enough flair?* Being in a constant state of comparison is not the best thing to help us cultivate our sense of inherent self-worth, which is the very opposite of comparison.

Let's use the concept of body image to dive more deeply into comparison. It's so easy to become self-critical especially when magazines plaster airbrushed Photoshopped images of what we're supposed to look like. Once upon a time we appreciated the imperfect body like Marilyn Monroe's. Photos of her show normal and beautiful curves complete with cellulite and ripples. Yet we celebrated mostly how she made us feel from the way in which she carried her body—as though there were nothing more beautiful. She radiated through her imperfections and we recognized it. Today our body-world plays by different rules.

So many of us know how difficult it is to feel good about our unique bodies and faces when we are held to images that are not real. It's bad enough to have to fight delusions in the mind about who we are, and now we add to it a battle against external illusions of altered bodies. We've got fast-food youth pills that come in the form of Botox, silicone, in-office facelifts, peels, laser facials, hair plugs, and steroids. We reconfigure our bodies with implants in some areas, and fat removal in others. We even take fat from one area and relocate it to another, always in search of the perfect configuration that makes us feel like we display the perfect picture. But how often does this story end with the feeling that finally *now* I'm perfect?

To make matters worse, new studies are even showing that individuals who use cosmetic procedures to freeze their facial muscles have a significantly impaired emotional perception compared to people who don't.[1] I am reminded of one of the scariest movies I remember from childhood: *The Stepford Wives*. It is a portrayal of a picture-perfect suburban community with fabulously gorgeous families wearing beautiful clothes, looking impeccable at social functions, and living the American dream. Even as a young child, this premise scared me more than any gory monster movie.

In the movie the women have been replaced with living doll copies that outwardly look perfect but inwardly have no ability to feel. The worst part is it was their husbands who replaced them! Seemingly, this makes the men's club very happy. Imperfection is considered a disease, and the remedy is to strip us of our most human qualities. The only thing that helped me get over this movie was the thought that this was fiction. As I look at life now, I have the eerie sense that some of us are living out this nightmare. How willing are we to sacrifice real emotional engagement with life for a flawless fake?

Are we becoming automatons in our unending search for perfection?

We've set up a constant quest for attaining something we're not and a persistent sense of "I'm not good enough." We fight hard to deny our genetics, giving up our own control over them to an outside fix. This is *not* a recipe for health. Masking the "I'm not good enough" thought by chasing an image doesn't change the fact that we're still feeling less-than on the inside as it eats away at our health and disposition. Our inner conflict is now a collective outer epidemic. Those emotional pain paths in our minds still activate, causing us to continually look for the next reprieve. But we can combat this epidemic of judgment and self-deprecation. I found a way to rebuild the foundation, and little by little, doing this every day has given me an innate gratitude for every inch of my imperfect and aging self. I've neurosculpted a way to feel good about myself in each moment, no matter what the external comparison point might be.

GRATITUDE CAN INFLUENCE THE BRAIN

Praise and gratitude is the great place from which to start building. The equation seems simple: neuroplasticity equals the hope of embracing something new, and hope can be a foundation of gratitude. So what's so important about gratitude? It is now believed that moments of expressed gratitude are linked to an increased secretion of oxytocin, a neurotransmitter in the brain that is highly involved in our perception of quality social bonding and trust.[2] Oxytocin is the neuromodulater women produce more of during pregnancy, childbirth, and nursing. This is a critical hormone involved in the effective bonding between mother and child. If expressed gratitude can bond us intimately together socially, what could it do for us when we express gratitude for ourselves? What could be different about your sense of self-worth if you cultivated this intimate relationship with your own being?

Talk is cheap when it comes to gratitude, so in order to cultivate it, we need methods and practices. I want to share this simple and effective practice, which was inspired by some observations I made at a local Korean bathhouse of women of all shapes and sizes. I had gone there to have a much-needed day of relaxation, but what I came away with was so much more. I think many women find a moment of awkward self-consciousness as they enter a room full of other naked women. Some women walked around quite comfortable in their skins, and some hurried about bent over, looking shamefully as though they had lost their cloak of invisibility. I found that I was uneasy looking at the uncomfortable women. My shoulders rounded and my eyes darted away in an attempt not to embarrass someone by looking at what they were trying to hide. Their discomfort was contagious.

But the opposite was also true. Those unashamed women who walked with proud and easy posture, whether they were naked or not, gave me permission to be present with my own body. Around these women, I didn't rush for my towel, or scurry from one place to the next. They didn't care to examine me in any sort of comparison. Their comfort level and disinterest in picking me apart gave me permission to do the same. I relaxed and enjoyed my time more.

I noticed an interesting custom. Women sat washing themselves on a row of seated and mirrored open showers. It was less like the shower ritual I was familiar with and more like they tended the temple of their bodies with scrub brushes or sponges, inch by inch. Each spent an eternity attentively making soapy swirls on every part of her body as though it were her mission and the only thing that mattered. Some women had their little girls there, emulating mommy in their clumsy attempts to be detail-oriented and thorough at an age when they could barely name all their body parts. This ritual seemed to take up to an hour. None of these women who were meticulously washing themselves looked at all uncomfortable in their skin.

I wondered: if each part of their body got that much attention, and nurturing, then maybe that was a way to cultivate this comfort or even reverence for one's own body. What does a body feel each time we contract and look away when it's naked? What would that same body feel if it stood tall and soaked up our own loving gaze when it was naked? I was determined to get more acquainted with my own body.

So the next time I went to the bathhouse, I tried bathing in a new way, spending what felt like far too long scrubbing each toe. What I noticed was that my mind had time to wander to mundane thoughts: What was I going to make for dinner? Who did I need to email? What bills didn't I pay? What debt was I in? These thoughts seemed like a waste of time. So instead of letting my mind continue to drift toward the negative and the never-ending to-do list, I began to focus on positive thoughts about my body during those times of meticulous care and attention. What could my intentional thoughts of gratitude and acceptance, combined with my own nurturing touch, do for my body, mind, and spirit? If people could heal the real neurological pain of a phantom limb by looking at an illusion in a mirror, surely I could have a profound effect on my body by looking at it and touching it while cultivating a mentality of care and nurture. How is looking in a mirror at an illusion any more powerful than looking at my own body with intention?

I felt renewed and more vibrant. I decided not to stop there. I took this practice home with me, adding it to my morning bathing routine.

What if you were to approach your daily shower or bath in a new way? Slow down just a bit, lather up just a little longer, and for each body part you wash, say or think one gratitude you associate with that part. Maybe it's something like:

- I am thankful for my strong arms that helped me carry my daughter.
- I am thankful for my wrists that are flexible and agile.
- I'm thankful for my hands that create so much, and for my fingers that enable me to communicate words on a keyboard.
- I am thankful for my belly and gut that digest and absorb nutrients to keep me healthy.
- I appreciate my chest that holds a space for my lungs and heart to be healthy.

When each shower becomes a gratitude ritual that combines physical motion of touching, nurturing, and washing away the old, we may begin to view our bodies differently. If we think about Hebb's Law of neuroplasticity,[3] which states that neurons that fire together wire together, then perhaps there's something very magical about this combination of physical action and mental focus.

NEURONS THAT FIRE TOGETHER

Pavlov's dogs are a perfect example of the concept of behavioral conditioning using Hebb's Law.[4] If you want a dog to salivate at the sound of a bell then you need to do two things: you need to make it salivate *while* making it hear a bell ring. When the bowl of food makes it salivate, the dog has a neurological excitation in a certain circuitry in the brain that correlates to its salivation response. The dog basically lights up the neural salivation map. If it simultaneously hears a bell, then it has an excitation in the auditory cortex in a map that correlates with the sound of the bell. When these two maps light up simultaneously, according to Hebb's Law, they begin to grow dendritic branches toward each other. Remember, dendrites are the spiny extensions of our neurons that connect to the axons of other neurons and enable an electrical charge to be sent across a gap via chemical messengers. Our dendrites are the mouthpiece in the telephone game of our thoughts.

If this simultaneous coupling of salivation and a bell sound happens with enough repetition, then the two maps reach toward each other and become linked. Eventually, if one side of the map in the dog's brain lights up—like the side that hears the bell—then a signal will excite the linked side that makes the dog salivate.

This is how neurons that fire together wire together. Maybe an even better example is when you smell that one smell you knew from childhood and you suddenly have full access to the memory or emotions associated with it. The neurological map of that smell signals the neurological memory map of any associated event because in the moment of creating that memory, those two things were coupled with a significant amount of attention.

Think about all the times you engage Hebb's Law without thinking about it. For me, I know I've coupled the mechanisms of operating a stick shift with the physical process of putting the key in the ignition. I see this very clearly when I'm driving an automatic car. As soon as I put the key in the ignition my left foot automatically tries to depress the clutch. I've wired these two functions together. It actually takes a moment of attention to undo that response.

Or maybe an even more subtle example rings closer to home for you: if you are someone who has money trouble or is in a dire financial situation you might notice over time that each time you open your checkbook or bank statement you have automatically pinched your eyebrows together or held your breath. Perhaps you've wired together a physical stress response with the action of opening certain pieces of mail. Perhaps this is so thoroughly wired that it is even subconscious.

Couldn't we use Hebb's Law to our advantage to unlearn a stress response or use an opportunity like our bathing ritual to practice gratitude? If we have a neurological response associated with the activity of washing ourselves, and we simultaneously practice realistic thoughts of gratitude for each motion, then over time won't we be linking these maps? Could we then elicit these feelings of gratitude each time we washed or touched our own body? Could we even begin to feel or embody that state of gratitude and self-acceptance simply by turning on the shower? Perhaps we could envision a time in which this type of practice results in people happy to be who they are, celebrating their unique gifts of physiology.

• • • • • • • • • • • •

DISCOVERY JOURNAL self-selecting the positive

We easily select negative images to focus on regarding our own bodies and physical appearances. For the next week keep a self-selection chart in which you intentionally select for positive images throughout your day. The chart below is an example.

Note what you feel like after one full week of creating positive body biases.

	Mon	Tues	Wed	Thur	Fri	Sat	Sun
Morning	Used my strong legs to take the stairs at work						
Afternoon	Gracefully carried two bags of groceries						
Evening	Maintained good posture during the movie						

Let's begin a practice of self-selecting for the positive rather than the negative, because we already know what focusing on the negative gets us. This is not an excuse to stop working toward bettering ourselves in the ways we want to; rather, it's a way to make that bettering process more loving, graceful, and perhaps even richer.

SCULPTING YOUR COMMUNITY

The ripple effect of change, hope, and transformation only works if there's a point of origination. A wave must originate somewhere at some source. YOU are that point of origin for waves of self-love and wholeness to ripple out to others. Assuming we are each equally capable origination points for this sort of positive change toward greater self-acceptance, what could each of us do to spread this effect? Knowing a little bit about the mirror neuron effect might help us broaden our understanding of our own power of influence in our environment. Although there is much to be learned about this phenomenon, there are some preliminary discoveries that make this concept quite exciting. Our brains possess certain networks of cells that activate when we perform certain functions and also activate *in the same way* when we observe others performing those functions. Think about your own brain for an instant. If there's a pathway in your brain that activates each time you smile, that pathway is linked to the *experience* of the smile. If that same pathway activates when you witness another person smile, then technically you've experienced that smile in just the same manner as if you smiled yourself. We have these mirror networks in different areas of the brain, and the speculation is that perhaps these are helpful in our ability to empathize, imitate, understand intentions, and learn languages. Some areas of our brain in which science has discovered these mirror neurons are the insula and anterior cingulate cortex. Both of these areas are involved in helping us process certain emotions and facial expressions like happiness and disgust.[5]

This discovery sheds light on a very interesting idea: we can't hope to change others until we first make those shifts in ourselves. Cultivating happiness on the inside can potentially affect others neurologically, perhaps even shifting their internal experience. In that way, your shower ritual has a ripple effect far beyond your immediate act. You cultivate a sense of contentment, joy, and even reverence for your body-world. You leave your house with a genuine smile on your face, a skip in your step, and a posture that radiates ease. Others in your close proximity register the emotions on your face and may begin to have neurological firing in their own brains that mirrors the experience of happiness and joy. Perhaps some of them even begin to smile and relax. And then they interact with others. This is the potential domino effect. It seems small at first, but then again so does every other small act before it ripples out.

The magical journey to glean information from the body-world begins with observations and listening. But this is just the start. If we stop there then we could even be worse off than if we didn't observe ourselves in the first place. I'm a huge believer in identifying our individual shortcomings or negative patterns, but I'm an even bigger fan of doing something with that information. I have many clients who come to me wanting to use neurosculpting to get a handle on various problems they're facing. Many of those clients first observe and notice how they are relating to the world and then they get even more excited about changing that pattern.

Remember the codependent student from the introduction—she did not act upon her observations and got stuck in old patterns. It's our duty and responsibility to act upon what we see, and then take action to effect our own internal change wherever possible. In this way, we become embodied examples of a nurturing and nurtured environment, and our thoughts can begin to move from criticism to acceptance, and eventually end up in gratitude, joy, and love. Those around us will sense that, and some of those people may even feel a shift of their own. We make bigger ripples with our resonance, not our theories.

. . . She told me to paint from my place of vibrancy. She reassured me that I could only create magnificent pictures, as I was a source of pure beauty. So I spit my cellular colors out onto a palette and began to paint on a blank canvas with my fingers: a foundation of electric silver, swirls of soft ice-blue, mountains of crimson and sunlight, and portals of colors beyond the visible spectrum. My painting was holographic, multi-spectral, and multi-dimensional. It began to lift off the canvas as though it had too much of its own life force to be contained. It began to form into a human shape with my exact dimensions, replicating me in the most resplendent ways.

She was beyond anything I'd imagined. The colorform before me turned around and, as she'd done before, she took two steps back-wards, bleeding her colors right through my skin, my muscles, my blood and bones until every inch of me drank her liquid light. I was full in both the creation and acceptance of what I could be. The Mother told me that I would always move through this world as this infinite and holographic masterpiece.

. . . .

PUTTING IT ALL TOGETHER cultivating self-acceptance

To embody the content of this chapter, try bringing the information into your daily life. As you review your first discovery journal exercise in this chapter circle three of the questions you will focus on this week.

1 Make some sticky notes to remind you to think about these at least once a day.

2 Put a reminder in your calendar or set your phone alarm to prompt you to think about these questions.

3 Make a commitment to journal about these questions each night before bed.

Write in the margins three different ways in which you will recognize the value of what you have to offer. Examples might be to speak one gracious thing about yourself each night before bed. Or maybe you'd like to circle some of your self-selected statements of positivity and put a star next to them so you can build on them the following week.

Lastly, do something fun!

1 Try making an abstract collage of yourself using only the most beautiful colors you can find.

2 You might even begin wearing clothing highlighting your favorite self-collage colors.

3 Give yourself some "you" time at least once a week to indulge in some low-cost activity that makes you feel good about yourself. This might be a long bath, a quiet walk around the neighborhood, or even an hour to listen to your favorite music uninterrupted.

6

memory, an attempt to make me believe

Memory, I realize, can be an unreliable thing;
often it is heavily coloured by the circumstances
in which one remembers.

KAZUO ISHIGURO

I had chosen a theme for this journey. It was time to clear out old stories of validation, in particular the need to be validated by men. The Mother told me it was possible to create a healthier way to relate to men, one in which I stepped outside of need and into camaraderie, so that some day I could walk side-by-side with a deep and resonant partner. It was time to stop chasing men as they casually tossed the breadcrumbs that I eagerly collected in their wake. She told me that in order to change, I had to first understand the nature of the fallible human memory.

I held on as she drew me back through time, counting down days as my past ticked by like quickly flipping photos. In my early twenties in my graduate studies, I pridefully debated with my professor so he would respect me and see that I understood him. Next, my late teens in my undergraduate studies, sitting conspicuously with my legs crossed, a spotlighted minority gender who was fond of wearing mini-skirts in a male-dominant engineering field. Then back to my early teens, noticing for the first time that the female body has the power to influence and turn heads. And as a preteen at the moment my brother's friend and neighborhood crush bought me a chocolate bar. Yes, at each moment, I had been noticed! The Mother stopped me here, frozen in time at the moment **he** handed me the chocolate bar. She pulled me out of the memory, leaving behind a chalked outline of where I stood.

"What are your thoughts?" she asked as she pushed my face to look at the hollow of my memory. My heart fluttered, and I couldn't help but feel the warm, coy flush of blood in my cheeks as I blushed. I was overwhelmed because he thought I was special, and I seemed to have his full attention. Butterflies danced around my stomach. I could not yet see where she was taking me.

She whisked me onward, back to my room outside of this body's lifetime. The more I visited, the more this room was home. I rolled down a plasma screen containing this lifetime's agreements. On it, my lessons were listed and detailed. I would choose to learn about valida-tion through my own self-compromise. I would choose to define my worth by chasing and catching men. I would choose to seek validation from men who were too contemptuous to give me consideration.

Then she asked, "What would it take for you to mark that line of the agreement 'completed' so you never have to repeat that lesson again?" I trembled. What if I never knew what it would take? I breathed deeply, drawing in some vapors from a well in the center of the room. The answer formed out of fragments and shimmers. What if I just chose to remember it all differently and recreate my history?

"Yes," she said.

And suddenly, it was time to go back . . . journeying up the ladder of time through the portal of birth, the reverse memories of re-membering as though it were happening for the first time, and not again. And in a blink, I was back to myself at twelve, being handed a chocolate bar from *him,* my neighborhood crush. This time I did not blush. My heart still raced, but not because *he* gave me anything. This new wave of innocent excitement seemed to be related only to the fact that I was about to eat chocolate!

I could no longer remember his name in this new version of what she told me was memory iteration 74. The Mother asked if I wanted to stamp this version as the newest, most accessible version—the one I'd recollect best. And so I did, allowing the joy of chocolate to be the context of the memory and watching the boy find equanimity with all the others as they blended into the scenery. "Are you ready to see the rest of your re-contextualized memories?" she asked.

As I sped back to my early teens, I noticed the power of the female body as it related to finding a purpose in life rather than power over others. I felt complete awe knowing that someday I'd create a life with this body. I traveled on to my late teens, taking a seat in class, ready to focus on my learning, not caring about my outfit. I suddenly appreciated how anonymity afforded me freedom as I chose comfort over provocative style. She took me further on to my early twenties, caring more about what moved me from literature and less about debating and proving it to my professor. Like a ripple through time, I realized the context of all memories can change . . . none of them are the truth of who we are. The Mother told me we get to choose the permutations of our recollections, as they are all just stories of make-believe.

I would forever know that each memory was an attempt to make me believe.

BUT I REMEMBER IT AS THOUGH IT HAPPENED YESTERDAY

It is a difficult pill to swallow when we are told our memories are only partly accurate. Memories are the anchor points of our own biography. They are the historical marks that put us at places in time with others, creating a web of interactions that hold together the story of who we are. We wear memories like badges, using them as guideposts or roadblocks. Each memory's trail creates life sculptures in the folds of our brain as we neurosculpt our reminiscences. Our identities are so wrapped up in our memories that we sometimes don't realize if we could just loosen that grip a bit we could be a bigger or better version of ourselves. Stepping into our greatness involves recognizing the past, and then contextualizing it in a way that allows us to grow into our present-time self fully.

As humans, we seem to be obsessively focused on the part of our lives that *already* happened rather than the parts that are happening right now. We look at photos to reminisce. Good friends often drift into reverie around the good old days. Parents try to hold on to memories as children grow up, slipping like sand through Mom and Dad's fingers. We reference memories of past injustices each time we meet similar circumstances. We hide behind images of long-ago days, and we mourn those who lose their ability to remember.

So what is this hold that memory has over us? And can neurosculpting give us back our power over ever-changing phantoms of what life used to be?

To be clear, our memories and past events have made each of us who we are in this moment, and for that I find it easy to be grateful. But until The Mother showed me I could place that memory on a shelf marked "done," I was unable to be in the present moment, unable to take in more of life because I filtered my experiences through outdated beliefs. Living in the present moment allows us to respond appropriately to situations with access to our full emotional spectrum rather than reenacting a well-played script for which we've already assigned our affected behavior.

I'm not suggesting we forget our pasts or deny the events of our lives. However, many of us keep pulling up the lens of our memories, and we use that lens in the present moment to filter life's experiences. I *am* suggesting that we honor the past by saying thank you and allowing it to retire into an area of our minds we can reference at any time but that does not cloud our present vision.

FOCUSED ATTENTION—MEMORY'S GLUE

Each of us thinks our memory is the accurate story, but neurologically, that's not the truth. To create a lasting memory the brain needs a few things in place. It needs to pay attention, and it needs an experience upon which to focus that attention, even if that experience is only in the mind's eye. It seems that our levels of attention during the experience are the critical factors in whether or not that event becomes well established in our memory. Because there are many different cortices of the brain involved in experiencing our reality, our memories are actually encoded as a synthesis of different parts or a construction of separate pieces. And the glue of this construction is focused attention.

Think about this scenario: if you are in a lecture or class, and you are distracted by some intrusive thoughts, remembering an argument you had that morning, multitasking on your phone while the teacher lectures, and shifting in your seat often because you are physically uncomfortable, you will remember far less of the lecture than if you paid full attention. Splitting attention uses valuable resources in areas other than to take note of the events we want to store in our memories. What is happening during those moments of full attention that allows an experience to be embedded?

Generally, moments of heightened attention correlate to a particular sweet spot of neurotransmitters in the PFC. Consider the analogy of a radio. When we want to tune in clearly to our favorite station and then program that station in, we need to lock on to the signal and simultaneously inhibit outside static, then commit it to a particular dedicated button. This is similar to what our neurotransmitters do when we are paying attention. Some of them, like norepinephrine, amplify the relevant signal while others, like dopamine, inhibit irrelevant static or distraction. And still others, like acetylcholine, help glue in the experience we've locked onto for quick and easy reference.[1] So when we feel ourselves paying attention, we are feeling this well-orchestrated harmony of stimulus amplification and inhibition of distractions.

There's yet another critical piece of this process that has the power to turbo-boost the glue of the newly forming memory, and that's our emotions. The more intensely we feel an emotion during the experience, the more attention we pay to the experience and the more deeply we embed the memory. In my dreamscape of memories it was clear that my attention was highly focused the moment I got the chocolate bar. I had a flood of emotional waves that caused me to stamp that memory into my biography's ever-accessible repertoire.

Fear is one of the strongest mapping emotions. Maybe this is an evolutionary gift to keep us from putting ourselves in harm's way too often. A good jolt of fear during an experience has the power to make that memory last an entire lifetime. Recall the spider story from chapter 2 and you can see how fear amplifies the process of creating and embedding memories.

Sadly, the more we use fear as a lens through which we view the world, the more fear makes a home in our memories. And if we layer version on top of version in our memories, the fear charge can bleed through to all other memories. This comes with the associated rise in stress hormones. Remember the story of the girl who was afraid of the spider. Her fear of the small event became a contagion that influenced her memories of camping in general rather than just that one moment. She elevated her stress hormones with each remembrance and caused her body to contract, prepare for action by impairing digestion and cognitive functioning, and reinforce this physical response pattern.

The process becomes even more complex as stress hormones impair our ability to relax. What science is now finding is that a period of brain rest after an experience is vital to our ability to store that memory more deeply. Remember, the hippocampus is an integral part of creating and storing our memories and is easily damaged by these very same stress hormones. This part of the limbic system plays a critical role in the creation of the episodic memory, but the storage of this memory over the long term involves translating the experience across to other structures of the brain, like the neocortex.[2]

It's not all bad news, though. Fear may be one of the strongest emotions in the process of embedding a memory, but fortunately it's not the only one. Novelty can hijack a moment, just like fear can, and cause us to pay full and heightened attention. Consider this example and you'll instantly understand the power of novelty in the memory process: Imagine you are in the same lecture as earlier—distracted and multitasking. The teacher's voice washes in and out like a droning hum. Suddenly, a miniature, three-inch purple baby elephant walks in to the room, stands in front of you and sneezes—the most adorable sound you've ever heard. What do you think the *one* thing is that you will remember from the lecture? You will likely remember the elephant indefinitely because it was a moment of total novelty, an unexpected yet nonthreatening stimulus that hijacked your scattered attention and recruited a moment of harmonizing neurotransmitter activity in the front of your brain. Your mind likely made you feel a moment of "huh, what's that?"

Now pretend you have a choice for a moment. Would you rather commit the vast majority of your life's experiences to memory through fear or novelty?

Once you've answered, understand that you *do* have a choice. Intentionally choosing moments of novelty over fear is possible with practice and dedication. The truth is that it's what we pay attention to and the way in which we choose to pay attention that defines the treasure chest of our biographical memories. And we can also lose our ability to retrieve a memory if we first experienced the moment in a state of divided or partial attention. So it's in our best interest to cultivate a practice and disposition that seeks to reframe an overreactive fear response to one of curiosity and novelty.

. . . .

DISCOVERY JOURNAL
shining light on the fear-based memories

Each of us has a set of standard default memories we tend to think about when we remember our childhood. In your journal, note the three most memorable fear-based ones and the three most memorable novelty-based ones. Examples might be the time you got into the car accident and the time you went on your first vacation. On a scale of 1 to 10, where 1 is a low level of emotion and 10 is a high level, note the level of emotion for each memory. You'll likely begin to see that the most easily retrievable memories have higher levels of emotional ranking.

Then try to remember the most mundane memory from your childhood, like the time you sharpened a pencil in third grade or the time you tied your shoe before going to school. Chances are you will struggle trying to elicit vibrant memories of these activities as they likely didn't have a strong emotional charge associated with them.

FIGMENTS OF OUR OWN IMAGINATION?

Hopefully you're beginning to see that we often go back to a canned set of default memories that came with a strong emotional charge and focus—but we don't reflect back on a big picture or the wholeness of our lives. What percentage of your total memories and experiences in life do you think this default set represents? In my case, I'll venture to say a small percentage of my life's experiences are stamped strongly. So when we think of our biography, we are usually referencing a sliver of what actually happened. How do you feel knowing that the bulk of your memories are like a limited set of television reruns from only a few of the many channels to which you have access? Couple this with the current idea that even *that* small percentage of memories is not accurate, and then this biographical picture becomes even less real.[3] Think about the times in which you and a friend were both present for the same event, yet heard yourselves describe it differently. These contrary reminiscences may have even sparked small arguments as you might recall trying to prove that your version of the memory was the correct one. Remember, the brain is a prediction machine so we color our experiences with what we expect to see. This can sometimes prevent us from being totally present, relying on our expectations to fill in the details rather than what's really happening. This is why two people experiencing the same event will have two different accounts for what happened.

Science has shown us that we are made up of more space than actual matter, and so too are our histories made up of more fiction or narrative than actual fact. We might just be figments of our own imagination!

THE PUZZLE PIECES OF OUR MEMORIES

Different aspects of our memories are stored in different areas of the brain simultaneously. For instance, we don't store the memory of how to ride a bicycle in the same place as our memory of the feelings we had opening our favorite birthday present. This specialized distribution acts as a way to distribute the memory so that later, when we reconstruct or consolidate it, we pull it back together from these different areas as a replay. Procedural memory, which includes all the things we needed to learn in order to ride the bicycle, is far more retrievable. This is so we don't have to think about those mechanical tasks. Could you imagine if you had to *try* to remember all the ways in which your body needed to adjust, compensate, and project spatial awareness each time you wanted to ride your bicycle? There's a reason the expression *it's just like learning to ride a bike* is used to indicate something you never forget. The expression sums up the power of our procedural memory recall.

Full memory retrieval is not like looking at a snapshot. It's more like creating a reconstruction of pieces and parts. When we think we remember exactly what happened, we're really creating a neurological rebuild or version of the event. Each time I remembered that day with my brother's friend and the chocolate bar I was actively building upon an early version. I was giving it more sticking power and credence, exercising its dedicated neurological activity. We encode our memories, with different levels of context and attention, and rebuild each one by filling in the gaps with a narrative to piece it all together seamlessly. This replay and consolidation tends to happen during our brain's rest time. So if we are impairing our ability to rest by flooding ourselves with gratuitous stress hormones, then we're setting ourselves up for impaired memory consolidation.

In fact, not a few minutes before sitting down to write this chapter, I heard my daughter and her friend argue about where she sneezed this morning. One remembered with full conviction that it happened in the bathroom, and the other remembered it to have happened on the stairs. Each had an entire story of context to debate and prove why she was right and the other was wrong. And this particular memory and event was only about one hour old!

When we think about our best self, the self that can rise above past limitations and embrace the present moment and evolve with it gracefully, then we are imagining a self that has learned to stamp outdated experiences as "done." This self we are hoping to be is the one who can be grateful for all the experiences we've had while being open to all the new ones inviting us to show up completely. To do this we need to create a practice that decouples the fear-based grip of the past from the memory of what once happened.

In case you're feeling the need to defend your own impeccable memory, here's a study to think about. In the *Journal of Consumer Psychology* in 2014, these results came to light: Three groups of people were exposed to popcorn ads.[4] One ad was low-imagery, one was slick with high-imagery, and the third group saw the slick ad and were given popcorn to taste during the commercial. One week later, those who watched the second, high-imagery ad—but had not tasted the popcorn—reported that they had tasted the popcorn. In fact, they were as likely to report that as the group that actually tasted it. The researchers called it "false experience effect," which builds on the principle that all memory, no matter how confident we are in it being real, is actually a reconsolidation of parts and pieces.

Imagery that engages emotional and social connections in the amygdala and hippocampus, in our fight-or-flight center, can result in the encoding of false memories that we stand behind as truth. If the brain can falsely believe we physically ate something that was never there, then surely you can understand that your memory of the details from a distant event could be flawed.

What do we want to do with all of this knowledge around our fallible memories? Surely we don't want this knowledge to cause us deep moments of insecurity and self-doubt. What if this basic information could become the context in which we look at all the past memories that are holding us back, and we look to free ourselves from the false hold they have on us? There's the potential for a great ethical debate around the art of rewriting unwanted or unhealthy memories. Maybe words like "denial" and "delusion" even come to mind.

But let's pretend for a moment that neither of these things are an issue. *If* our inaccurate memories keep us locked in negative patterns, and we know that each time we remember a particular experience we actually reconstruct the event rather than have the first iteration's experience of it, then wouldn't it be beneficial to change our *relationship* to the negative stories as a way to improve our health, mental disposition, behavior, and well-being? Wouldn't it be beneficial for everyone to move out of unwarranted fight-or-flight patterns? What if you could squeeze all the richness and vitality out of your experiences and program *that* into your memories, so that each time you remembered it was with vivid detail? What would you choose to hold on to? This is not an argument for erasing memories and shirking responsibility for the lessons that came with the memories, but it is a proposal that if we were to find a new relationship to the context of the memory, then we might be able to find some healing and expansion for the mental, physical, emotional, and spiritual bodies. I understand this concept can be difficult to come to terms with. How dare I insinuate that the important and life-shaping events in your life are partly imagined! Believe me, I wrestled with this like a ninja. How could science be telling me that the traumatic events in my life were simply my own twisted interpretation? So rather than get stuck in this battle that disempowered me and minimized my own very real emotions, I chose to view it like this instead: *Real or not, my memories have shaped me into the person I am today, and for that I honor their validity—but they do not have to act like scripts that limit my potential from this day forward.* What would happen to our interactions with others if we cleaned up all the pieces of ourselves held captive by our unhealthy memories and were able to access our full potency in each moment?

How does one do this exactly? Each person will renegotiate their life's memories differently. Here is an example of how one of my students renegotiated hers in an attempt to loosen the grip of the past and become more present.

Jane's earliest memory was from a traumatic experience she had at fifteen months old. She recalled the sight of a huge concrete slab and the sound of a very loud bass drum that caused her to cry a lot that day. Jane had been seeing a therapist and in a counseling session realized the reason this memory imprinted so profoundly was due to its close proximity to a car accident a few weeks later in which her parents were severely injured. Jane noted these two traumatic experiences mapped so deeply into her biography and brain that her life's rhythm was disrupted by bouts of depression about every sixteen to eighteen months.

When Jane began using neurosculpting practices to rewrite her limiting beliefs, she learned that her brain's response to stress was to tell her body to freeze, much like mine did. Jane had a hypervigilant vagus nerve response as well. This condition defined her permissions throughout life, causing her to miss out on activities and experiences for fear of engaging her freeze response. Over the years together we worked on ways to decouple the freeze response from her memories and history, identifying and separating out the physical pattern from the memories. Jane's original story was, "I was traumatized as an infant, and this affects how I navigate stressful situations." With years of a practice she's told me her new story is "When I was traumatized as an infant, my mother took care of me. I am safe, supported, and nurtured." She currently feels safe and confident doing things she used to avoid, and hasn't experienced a cycle of depression since. Jane didn't erase her traumatic memories. She chose to use them in a different context, and in doing so opened herself up to healing and freedom from self-limiting traumatic stories.

• • • • • • • • • • • •

DISCOVERY JOURNAL **renegotiating a memory**

Go back to the fear-based memories you noted earlier. Note what part of the memory you focused on each time you recalled it.
Examples are:

- I focused on the unfairness of the situation.
- I focused on the element of surprise.
- I focused on the fear that if I were hurt, I might never recover.
- I focused on blaming the other person.

Now note at least one other novel context for the memory that could become a new point of focus.

Examples include:

- I could focus on the fact that I actually came out
  of that event safely.
- I could focus on the other person's perspective
  and intentions.

As you begin to reframe your memory contexts, you can begin recollecting these memories with a new focus that recognizes even more depth to the events that occurred.

If you renegotiated your fear-based memories in this way would you still need the approval of others to the point of compromising your own ethics, or could you be grounded in your own guiding principles? I knew if I stayed locked up in a maze of painful masquerades, I'd always just be shades of my total potential. So how can we embrace our full potential?

When I was pregnant I desperately wanted to create a safe environment for my baby to grow in. The Mother told me I needed to make room by removing some of the deep stored pain to make sure my child didn't develop in that environment. She told me it was my responsibility to do the clean-up if I were bold enough to create a living being. So at a few weeks pregnant, she called me forth to confront some fractured and barbed pieces of myself.

She led me into a room soft with the sweetest colors, warm and insulated with whispers and caresses. I had never been here before, and I didn't want to leave. There was peace and ease. I was just me. The Mother indicated for me to get comfortable, as I was about to have a visitor. A door opened and a young version of myself walked in sheepishly . . . me at a point in time in which I chose to buy in to a crushing fear of my own potential. A me who chose to believe I was not worthy and had to mask myself to be accepted. A me who compromised my own values to appease parasites and predators. A me who wanted to be invisible. A me who would be half-present for the daughter I was creating in my body.

I looked upon myself without judgment, and a wave of compassion welled from a place deep inside a bottomless ocean. I asked, "Why?" This young me answered, "Closing up was the only way I knew how to cope with the sharp edges of my broken and incomplete pieces." The Mother motioned for me to touch the young replica shivering in my presence. I reached out and hugged her, feeling her small bones in my arms. I heard myself tell her how much I appreciated all she had tried to protect for me. I thanked her for being brave enough to hold tightly all these years to the masks she thought I needed to hide behind. I told her it was all right for her to be a child once again—because as a woman, I could handle the memories she was trying to shield me from.

We looked at each other, in mirrored eyes, for a lifetime—and then she ran off to play. A whoosh of pressure burst out of my chest, and like a swarm of butterflies mask after mask fluttered out of my heart in a cloud of colors. All of my vaudeville faces swirled off into the distance, leaving me with just a gaping hole where my insides used to be. I began to tremble as the real question grew louder and more ominous with each held breath . . . "Who am I without my masks? Who am I without her?" I simply did not know how to **be** when I stood naked with myself.

One by one, each painful memory I attempted to shield from rose up for my review before I put it back into the vacancy of my being. Would I put it back the same way, or would I shift the context to be grateful for the lesson and take back a piece of my own strength in the renegotiation?

So, piece by piece, I chose seniority over each moment, filling myself with an unmasked strength until I was bigger than I'd ever been. The Mother disappeared so I could cry alone. I felt free, empowered—and I finally felt like a woman who knew who she was. With my limiting memories renegotiated, I felt capable of nurturing the growing child inside my womb, having just taught myself how to do so.

You never have to have experiences with The Mother like I did to begin to realize that your own constructed biography can be renegotiated at any time. This will enable you to show up more fully in each moment. Piece by piece, you can take each of your most limiting memories and look at them in the light of their own room for growth and evolution. Although your relationship to them feels real, it doesn't have to continue in the same manner. As soon as you make the decision to create a new relationship with a memory, your neurology gets to participate in an electrical and chemical remapping.

PROGRAMMING A NEW CODE . . . ALL DAY LONG

We program ourselves all the time, often reprogramming old code by rehashing old versions of our memories. So how do we take all that theory and put it into real-time use? What if we were to take our skill of unconscious programming and make it conscious? We're doing it all day long anyway!

Remember how powerful novelty can be to help us map. We can use this to our advantage. This is possibly my favorite part of neurosculpting! Each time your mind says, "huh?" to a benign stimulus, like it did with the miniature elephant, you are in a mappable moment with your attention centers recruited and focused. What if you were to combine those key mapping moments with a new idea, a new belief, some dopamine-stimulating comedy and laughter, or a new story? Couldn't we then begin creating and recalling a new story in the context of that symphony of neurotransmitter glue so that new storyline embeds more deeply?

You can have lots of fun with creating these mapping moments. Here's the key: *during* each of these novel activities, when your attention centers are steeped in a rich learning environment, think of a belief about yourself or your life that you'd like to strengthen, or you can reference the memory of a happy or relaxed time.

Here are twenty of my favorites:

1 Brush your teeth with your nondominant hand.

2 Use your nondominant hand to stir things when you cook.

3 Squeeze the shampoo bottle with the opposite hand.

4 Fold your laundry in a different way.

5 Rearrange your drawers.

6 Choose a new route to work.

7 Hold your car keys in the opposite hand.

8 Turn your coffee cup so the handle is on the opposite side.

9 Walk around the opposite side of the car when pumping gas.

10 Brush your hair with your opposite hand.

11 Remember your funniest stories at least once a day, or watch something that gives you a real belly laugh.

12 Take a laughter yoga class.

13 Have someone you trust walk you around by the arm while you keep your eyes closed.

14 Use the nondominant leg to start your climb up or down the stairs.

15 Choose a different seat at the dinner table.

16 Sleep on the other side of the bed.

17 When clasping your hands, position your fingers
in a unique way.

18 Count your money with your nondominant hand.

19 Water your plants with your nondominant hand.

20 Reverse the order of your morning face washing
and teeth brushing routine.

Here's what I have found to be the result of years' worth of this mapping practice: I am now selectively choosing at multiple times throughout my day to focus on better and healthier stories, reinforcing positivity while doing something novel and non-threatening. I can retrieve those stories more easily, and now they feel like familiar memories. I interrupt my negative default patterns at many points in my daily cycle, down-regulating my negativity bias. Some of my positivity scripts are gratitude based like:

- I'm so grateful I'm healthy enough to work today.
- I'm grateful I have a stable home with food in
  the refrigerator.
- I'm grateful to be able-minded and able-bodied enough
  that such a small annoyance is the focus of my attention.
- I'm grateful I have the resources at my disposal to hone
  my skills in . . .

The practice reinforces the ability to reframe, renegotiate, and create new patterns that stick.

• • • • • • • • • • • •

DISCOVERY JOURNAL **identifying your positivity scripts**

Note at least two or three key statements or beliefs you will use
in your novelty remapping regimen. Identify which of the novel

exercises you'll do this with from the list of twenty I gave you, or identify a few original ones that work better for you. Write one or two new statements each week to add to this regimen. Notice how quickly thinking better thoughts comes during each of these novel moments.

• • • • • • • • • • • • • •

PUTTING IT ALL TOGETHER
cultivating freedom from the past

Some of us have skeletons in our closets or painful pasts that we are not well equipped to deal with. I was one of these people. Maybe you're familiar with trying to hide infidelity like I was, or wearing a mask of righteousness to hide indiscretions. I have been both the liar and the one lied to—the one cheated on and the cheater. One of the things I found most helpful in freeing myself from the fear-hold my memories had over me was to be gentle with myself and start working with the manageable memories. As much as I wanted to jump in and clean up all of my stories, I needed first to create a strong foundation of forgiveness and acceptance for myself.

A teacher once told me that I came into her program with a platter of garbage, and I wanted to dump it all at once. I couldn't have agreed more. She then said, "You know, you could do that with pain and punishment, or you could do that with ease and grace. Either way, you'll get it done." Ease and grace? That was a new concept for me, and some of you might also find that concept unfamiliar as well.

As you integrate this information, please be accepting of your own mistakes. As you go back through this chapter to highlight areas of importance or make notes in the margins with your nondominant hand, take some time to savor and sit with the information before expecting to heal all of your past. Revisit your Discovery Journal exercises over and over, trying them on different memories until each feels complete. If you have old photos, you may want to take some time to choose a few that represented you at a time in life you'd like to put in the past. You can look at these photos as you work with the second journal exercise in this chapter. You may even want to rearrange your photo albums with new titles such as "Lessons Learned." In this way, you can recategorize memories that have a hold on you as *done, filed,* or *in the past.*

After you've digested this concept of what our memories can do, and find that some of your discoveries revealed the need for more accountability on your part, you can even make efforts to apologize to those you've wronged, no matter how long ago it was. This action can sometimes be helpful in stamping that memory as completed. In this way, as we free ourselves up from the hold of the past, we create more space and energy. Do you want to fill in all that space with fear—or with love?

7

love versus fear

Trusting is dangerous.
But without trust there is no hope for love,
and love is all we have to hold against the dark.

RIAN MALAN, *My Traitor's Heart*

This time, she took me to another life, a space in time to which I was still attached. "But what if I don't believe in past lives?" I said. The Mother told me that it didn't matter. I could call it whatever name I wanted; there was a storyline underneath it all that kept me imprisoned. She told me if I needed to believe it was a subconscious creation or if I chose to believe it was a past life, the result was the same. If I wanted to find out how to love, I'd need to tie up the loose ends of these tethers. She pulled me out of my skin to travel faster, and in the blink of an eye and the passing of eternity we stood on a cliff's edge in Corsica. I had never been there, but the rocky cliff under my feet was familiar. The crescent alcove of beach far below was a space I remembered, a place I shook to think about. The smell of the ocean was home. The small stone-and-wood cabin behind me knew my scent and the shape of my frame in its door.

I had come back. The bench outside had supported me many times as I ate olives, almonds, and honey. I didn't want to be on the edge of the cliff, because I knew she was about to show me what was below. We climbed down. I was adept, remembering all the times I'd done this before. The sand underneath my feet was soft and fine. The Mother showed me snippets, flashes in my mind that filled in the small empty spaces. I remembered it—his breath so close to my face—and I shook.

"You are holding on to blame and anger. You must let it go if you want to find love," she said.

And on the trails of those words came the clarity of the two bodies in the sand—me as a young boy, about six years old, and my father with his flaming eyes. I noticed the strange trail my clubfoot made in the sand, my unique signature, as he dragged me to the water's edge. He was big and heavy, and the weight of his knee crushed my chest when he pinned me down. His burning eyes seemed to look beyond me as his hands tightened on my throat.

It was not my fault my mother died in childbirth, or that my deformed foot prevented me from contributing the way any boy should. It was not my fault my father was an angry alcoholic spiraling into a cascade of failure stories. Yet I knew that I was to blame, and he'd see it no differently. I was a painful reminder of all he'd lost and all he'd never be. I turned my head just enough to look at the ocean as he squeezed any last trace of breath out of my burning lungs. The waves came. And when he let go, the ocean washed me away.

The Mother told me I had a choice: to hold on to his fiery eyes as I had been doing in this current lifetime with the version of him who accompanied me into this incarnation, or to let them go and give them up to the earth's waters. Would I stay in fear, or could I move into forgiveness and know love? I was small and alone on that beach, but the ocean swept in and washed away the remnants of his face and replaced my last memories with a cool and cleansing touch. I couldn't love him, but I could recognize he did his dysfunctional best as fear took his manhood down. The ocean, I was told, makes everything all right.

CAN WE NEUROSCULPT LOVE?

It is interesting for me to talk about love versus fear. I feel very equipped to speak about fear, and I sometimes feel like a charlatan when I speak about love—mostly because in my own story of myself, I didn't always show up as an unconditionally loving character. Yes, I love deeply and strongly . . . adamantly, in fact. But I tend to reserve that effusive openness for a select few nearest to my heart. I've hoarded and rationed love, kept it greedily away from those on my periphery. I don't associate myself with the imagery of a set of indiscriminately open arms longing to hug any stranger who walks by. I needed to be coaxed into affection, feeling a sense of paralysis around soft touch. As a young girl I was quite comfortable delegating my desires to vivid fantasies I kept in my head while I remained cool and aloof on the outside. I played it so cool, in fact, that when I flew across the Atlantic that summer after saving up for years and fantasizing about my first love, I couldn't even reach out to hold his hand unless he made the gesture first.

So when I think of love like I've seen in movies or read about in books, or as in the kind described by the monks I studied with, I think of someone who can give it freely to everyone. To speak of it in *that* sense would make me a fake, so I am only going to speak about love as I know it—in small and ever-healing pieces that have only given me a glimpse of how much more there is to learn. I am speaking as someone who is learning how to have and give more of it. I have learned that I can either subconsciously support my fear-based stories and keep myself from deeper expressions of love and stuck in a freeze response, or I can intentionally sculpt new stories that override the fear and open myself to new depths of love's experience. We don't have to wait for love to hit us over the head and proclaim demonstratively that it's safe now; we can do the work to be open and ready to recognize it in places we wouldn't have thought of before.

JUDGMENT IS FEAR'S COUSIN

I felt judgmental growing up, cynically making assessments of others' dispositions and motives. In fact, I spent too much time considering the motives and impulses of those around me. Often I was right, which resulted in my becoming the unofficial therapist for all of my friends. My observations seemed to make sense to them and give them clarity. They perceived me as loving and caring. Back then, the position of listener and healer didn't come from an altruistic desire to help, but it came more from a need to be right about the judgmental way in which I saw people. I was in fear most of the time of being abandoned, discounted, or dismissed. I used fear as a motivation to prove my worth. In truth, I was sweet and considerate, empathic and diplomatic, but I never *felt* I understood what loving unconditionally meant.

There are some children who run into a room and initiate a hard embrace with family or friends. There are those kids who like to squeeze each other so hard they could burst. I used to see little girls at school reaching for each other's hands to skip along. I remember commercials of best friends, arm in arm, sharing light-hearted smiles. I was not like that. I never felt safe enough or trusting enough to risk initiating an act like that. What if it were turned down? I was reserved, internalized, and I felt most comfortable in my own space. I was the recipient of affection, never the initiator.

Demonstrative acts of loving affection like holding hands, giving deep hugs, or even touching someone's shoulder while speaking to them were unsafe for me. So my expression of connection came through my words. Even as a small child, this fear-filter constricted me uncomfortably. I couldn't let anybody in more than part way, so I remained aloof in my head and told myself I was an observer rather than a doer. In this way, I didn't have to love or connect; I was too busy observing—too busy judging. In order for me to feel comfortable with my own limitations I needed to condemn the opposite in others, or call out the vices of those around me. Perhaps this was a way for me to feel some twisted sense of company in my fortress of emotional constriction.

This is the relationship to love that I chose to renegotiate. I was tired of all the missed opportunities for deeper connection. One day my best friend from childhood told me she felt she knew very little about me because I was always so guarded. I saw her have deeper relationships with new friends than with me after a lifetime spent together.

I didn't want to feel as if I was moving through life alone, so I took The Mother's wisdom to heart and paid close attention to my vision.

You might not be like me at all. Maybe the love relationship you'd like to renegotiate is the opposite of mine, where you've lavished affections and love, time and energy onto too many in the hopes of feeling accepted or loved back. Your story of love might involve a martyr-like dynamic in which you've sacrificed at your own expense to the point of depletion. Maybe you've found yourself throwing your affections at anyone who stopped long enough to catch them. This, too, can be renegotiated.

The Mother had shown me in my meditations that I had some underlying storyline implying that it was dangerous to love . . . deadly, actually. This served to protect me in my youth, to keep me safe and vigilant where others might be vulnerable. But continuing on like that in adulthood became limiting and lonely. So what does one do with their own limitations once they find out they are outdated, out of place, and out of time? What limiting and fear-based stories are keeping you from fully giving and having love?

• • • • • • • • • • • •

DISCOVERY JOURNAL the "why" behind fear and love

If you are a withholder like I was, note and describe a few times in which you felt the desire to connect more deeply with someone, but held yourself back instead. This can be an instant with a stranger in need, when you continued to walk by instead of help like you wanted to, or this can be an example in a deep and cultivated relationship. At the end of each noted time, write the prompt "Why?" and see if you can answer that truthfully. Next to that answer, note what you would need to overcome in order to have acted upon your desires. If you are an indiscriminant giver of love, then note and describe a few times in which you felt you sacrificed too much of yourself to please another, and ended up depleted and with a sense that you weren't loved back. At the end of each description, write the prompt "Why?" and see if you can answer that truthfully. Next to that answer, note what you would need to feel inside of yourself in order to have acted more for your own sense of fulfillment.

NEURAL MECHANISMS OF LOVE

Maybe you are getting a sense of your own patterns around freely loving, or gratuitously loving. Do your "whys" come from a place of fear or a sense of judgment? We know that when our fight-or-flight center is engaged as a result of our fear-based stories, we recruit blood and glucose to that part of the brain to feed its continued activity. The more we practice recruiting resources and fuel to the limbic center, the more we train that center to respond and maintain dominance. When we allocate our valuable fuel to the limbic center, we are recruiting it partly from the PFC. In a sense, amping up the limbic system down-regulates the PFC. If you are spending time in your fear-based thoughts, then you can't possibly have an easy time accessing an open and loving state because you've limited the brain's ability to experience compassion and love, as they tend to correlate to activity in the PFC. (I am making a distinction here between open and compassionate loving and physically heated loving.) As much as we'd like to hope, we can't actually be loving and open while simultaneously activating fear, judgment, and limitation. We might find a way to quickly dance between the two if we're skilled enough, but we can't do them simultaneously. Think about it. Can you simultaneously be in a state of condemnation and unconditional love? Can you be swept away by love and have a sense of imminent threat or danger at the same time?

In a very real sense, my fear-based stories entrained my brain into a precedent mode or a dysfunction. I taught myself selective negative bias, as most of us easily do. I taught myself how to contract around gestures of love, how to withhold vulnerability, and how to insulate myself behind a fortress. We can use neurosculpting to reshape the underlying fear-based thoughts that cause our own sense of limitation or judgment, and create a new and different relationship to that fear—one that would no longer activate our limbic response.

What exactly is so important about creating a healthy relationship to both giving and receiving love? It can be a platform from which to create lasting and healthy social bonds, and also vastly influence the health and well-being of our mind, body, and spirit. Creating a healthy relationship to love is vital in our quest for healing and wholeness. In fact, love is the fast track! Diane Ackerman writes:

> James Coan, a neuroscientist at the University of Virginia, conducted experiments in 2006 in which he gave an electric shock to the ankles of women in happy, committed relationships. Tests registered their anxiety before, and pain level during, the shocks.
> Then they were shocked again, this time holding their loving partner's hand. The same level of electricity produced a significantly lower neural response throughout the brain. In troubled relationships, this protective effect didn't occur. If you're in a healthy relationship, holding your partner's hand is enough to subdue your blood pressure, ease your response to stress, improve your health and soften physical pain.[1]

What if a healthy relationship with love could help you modulate everything from your autonomic nervous system responses to your sense of belonging in the world? Wouldn't it be worth it to spend more time cultivating it?

When I was younger I didn't spend nearly as much time cleaning up my stories around love as I did repeating the same old pattern with love. Did you ever wonder why that new relationship ended up looking just like the last one? When the patterns don't work for your best sense of well-being, then it's time to look at why. According to science, healthy love has neural connections to our sense of bonding by increasing the neurotransmitter oxytocin, fondly known as our bonding/trust molecule. It can spike our sense of reward by activating our dopamine centers—the very same centers that become active with certain addictive drug use. And healthy love can down-regulate our limbic stress and fear response.[2]

The Mother showed me in my vision on the beach that in order to have all of these benefits of healthy love and find my way to wholeness I needed to learn how to forgive and detach. Ah, familiar advice: "Just let go." But how could I do this in my day-to-day life?

NEUROSCULPTING FORGIVENESS

In order to forgive I had to actually stop judging! Forgiveness, for me, was a learned brain process. As someone who could easily spend too much time in my internal spaces, it became easy to replay events with great detail. The negative events in my life played out in my head, over and over again, each time crystallizing with more clarity. I could blame each person involved more fully each time I rehashed my version of the story. I could reenact moments of vindication and feel victorious at someone else's expense. I could repeat a story so much that sometimes I'd work myself into more highly charged emotional states than the actual event elicited. Does any of this sound familiar to you?

The Mother taught me that I could use the very same internal spaces to let all of that go, rather than make it stick. How much better would you feel if, after a terrible interaction, closing your eyes enabled you to forgive the person rather than continue the blame loop? The issue for me was I didn't have the *desire* to forgive in these internal spaces. Instead, I had an unconscious drive to marinate in the thick of it, finding validation and justification around every turn. What was the fuel of this drive?

The stress and fear cycle is usually accompanied by a buzz from the adrenaline that's kicked up. The drama helps us feel alive, engaged, alert, and sometimes even productive. Can you relate to those times in which you became outraged by someone and suddenly you had more energy than you had before? If you're violent, like I was, then maybe you understand the tidal wave of emotions that well up during a fear or judgment moment that give you the uncontrolled impulse to throw an object, or punch a wall. Much to my dismay, I've had a few relationships in which I left my mark both emotionally and through physical destruction. I once had a boyfriend who had to cover the holes I made in his walls with posters! Even though we may be ashamed of this after the fact, the truth is this surge of adrenaline can become addictive because it makes us feel powerfully alive. Eventually, the body needs to rest or restore in a come-down process. This can feel exhausting, make us less social, and even make us want to retreat. How does exhaustion feel in comparison to a surge of adrenaline? Once we get into this drama cycle we can actually default to spike our adrenaline simply to feel that buzz. For me, none of this was conscious. I hated feeling like a zombie after a big argument. This recovery time of exhaustion, antisocial behavior, and reclusiveness isn't very supported or encouraged by society. Naturally, many of us try to avoid that by spiking into fear or judgment again.

So, instead of allowing the restoration process to take its natural course, we avoid it. We choose instead to spike ourselves back into an energized state by sparking up more drama, stress, or fear. This self-perpetuating process can feel like a drama addiction. In fact, I'm betting you've heard yourself label others at times as "drama queens." Maybe *you've* even been labeled that way. But this cycle doesn't have to continue. My vision told me it was possible to forgive even the most heinous act, so I trusted there was a way. As my mind got in my way locking me into my patterns, I had to look to what my body could do to help shift it.

. . . .

DISCOVERY JOURNAL is it time to forgive?

In your journal, note one or two of the bigger events that seem to have you stuck in a state of judgment, bitterness, fear, or some other profoundly negative emotion. Describe the event. Underneath the description write the heading, "What Would Happen If I Forgave?" Make a list of the things you think might be different about your own life and body state if you took your invested energy back from this event. You might note things like:

- I'd spend less time rehashing the details and have more time for . . .
- I would stop grinding my teeth at night.
- I might sleep better.
- I would stop getting angry each time I heard that person's name.

Notice how many items you can list that could change based on this one forgiveness.

SUPPORTING LOVE AND
FORGIVENESS VIA THE BODY

Remember, in this path of mind, body, and spirit we can't ignore the body as a source of teaching and healing. I have found that what I eat, how much I sleep, and the rigorous way in which I actively pay attention to sculpting a new story all greatly enhance my brain's ability to let go and detach. My new patterns disable this drama-addiction loop and free me to cultivate moments of restoration and hormonal homeostasis. If we could move ourselves into a healthier way to eat in order to support the functioning of the PFC over the limbic response, then maybe we could fortify ourselves with the foundation we need to access our higher spiritual capabilities—like forgiveness. I think of an athlete when I think of this process. In order to win a race, an athlete cultivates both mind and body in order to have the focus and execution necessary. We, too, need to listen to both mind and body to have the determination and resilience necessary to execute the higher-level skills of detachment and forgiveness.

So can we find forgiveness and love through good diet, sleep, and physical and mental exercise? That seems a bit of a stretch, but the logic lends itself to the idea that *if* we are putting into our bodies what the prefrontal cortex *needs* to be at its prime, it might be able to bring those attributes online that much more easily. Let's remind ourselves what some of those PFC attributes are: forgiveness, empathy, introspection, self-reflection, problem-solving, big-picture thinking, language, self-motivation, goal-setting, focused attention, and even moments of insight.

If we have underlying stories that make it feel unsafe to express or receive love and forgiveness, and we couple that undercurrent with poor food choices that contribute to dominance of our fear center, do you see how difficult it would be to change? Doesn't it make sense that skewing the odds in this fear-based way makes us less likely to openly embrace change and growth? But now that we know that it doesn't have to be this way, it behooves us to do something about it. Neurosculpting puts the process in place to begin encoding a new undercurrent storyline while fueling on foods and nutrition that can enhance the very processes necessary to encode a new map.

WHAT'S LOVE?

This is a loaded question! I'll invite you in to question it and discover your own answers as we talk about love. Through my own practice of neurosculpting, I've come to know more about love, step by step. For me, love equates to feelings of safety, and the inclusion and belonging I feel when being acknowledged. I've been in plenty of relationships where these two things were missing, and no matter how much chemistry there was between us, I had a hard time feeling and giving love. As a child, I was grounded and thrived when I was safe. I searched for Mommy's embrace when I was hurt, I hid behind Daddy's leg when I met strangers, and I knew I'd be tucked in at night by loving hands. A child can thrive in different ways when she doesn't have to spend her resources worrying about food, shelter, and safety. When we are not safe we need to rely on our fight-or-flight center to navigate the world. Remember, having this as the dominant navigating system actually can inhibit our experiences of compassion and forgiveness. Maybe you define safety differently than I do. But I'm sure we can agree that if we had to spend most of our time in primitive survival-threat mode we'd have less time and inclination to ponder how others might feel, to let our guard down, or to risk being vulnerable. I found all of these necessary for me to forgive and love more deeply.

A sense of belonging and acknowledgment does wonders for an individual's sense of worth and being loved. It's far easier to give and receive love when we belong to a supportive group or tribe than when we feel like an outcast or loner. Neuroscience has discovered that when our sense of inclusion or relatability is threatened, the brain easily defaults to limbic threat mode and we begin to up-regulate the stress process. In fact, exclusion by strangers is enough to cause pain and the brain to perceive its fundamental needs are threatened.[3] So we know that our sense of being loved, and even giving love, has something to do with our ability to feel safe and as though we are a part of a community. These are the very things we undermine in ourselves when we cut ourselves off from healthy social connections and choose to perceive others with judgment.

Neurologically, love also has something to do with the corresponding activity of oxytocin in the brain. This neurotransmitter is affectionately called the "trust and love" hormone. Remember, its activity is high during sexual reproduction, childbirth, and nursing. It's a critical chemical that helps us bond with our loved ones. There are even experiments done with voles that show a relationship between a vole's level of oxytocin and their monogamous or polygamous status.[4]

So, if an increase in oxytocin helps us bond better, trust more, and even commit to lifelong monogamy, does that mean love is a chemical reaction? I hardly think so, but I can't deny that the health of my brain affects my ability to express and feel love. But we all know it's not just the brain and chemicals involved in love, it's the heart as well.

HEAD VERSUS HEART

Some people perceive the heart as the central point of love. Ancient civilizations believed that the heart was the central intelligence in the body, and therefore the guiding force of the experience of love. Modalities like HeartMath use research that demonstrates the magnetic field of the heart as a powerful force that can influence our own brain waves, and the brain waves of individuals in our close proximity.[5] I know personally that I've also experienced love with my heart as the center point at times. I recall finding it hard to breathe and feeling flutters of both heart and stomach when that special someone caught my eye. I'm sure you can associate with those emotions that come with the end of certain relationships. Don't we often say our *heart* was broken? We could get into a very long conversation in which we are trying to prove where love lives, as though that were really even possible. Haven't you found yourself in conversations where you are explaining your conflict because your head wants one thing but your heart wants another? There are the heart supporters, and there are the neuro-supporters. And because we are lucky enough to have science involved in researching both it seems fair to say both have a huge influence in how we experience love! Maybe now we can drop the head *versus* heart debate and begin talking about the head *and* heart partnership. We can't evolve when we hold stories of fear in the mind and then try to command the heart to open. Nor can we evolve when the mind desires love but the heart is closed and shielded. As we rewrite our limiting stories, heal, and evolve into our sense of wholeness we are doing so because we are creating a language that allows both head *and* heart to speak in the same terms so conflict melts away. In my vision I held anger, judgment, and fear in my mind, and as a result I couldn't find a safe way to open my heart. These two miraculous organs have the ability to open doors of love and connection and transform our lives when they work together. What does the dialogue look like between your heart and head?

• • • • • • • • • • •

DISCOVERY JOURNAL your head-versus-heart debate

Note a few of the times in which you found yourself stuck in a debate between your heart and your head. Note the mental conversations or even real conversations you had as you were deciding in favor of one or the other. Note if you used your head to make the final decision, favoring logic, or if you used your heart to make it, favoring your emotional pull. At the end of each description, begin a sentence with this prompt: "What would it have taken for this particular debate to be resolved gracefully? What would it have taken for my heart and head to listen to each other?" See if you can answer this prompt. Don't worry if you can't. Simply asking yourself the question will open a new line of thought around what might have felt like a clumsy stalemate. Perhaps you could ask yourself those questions next time you find yourself debating between heart and head.

The first step in creating a dialogue between head and heart is in identifying their voices as you've begun to do in the journal exercise. In my own marriage of heart and head I've taken it slowly, allowing each part of me to inform the other in manageable chunks that begin to make sense to me over time. I am still not the girl who runs into everyone's arms. I'm still not the girl who grabs for my best friend's hand. I'm not the girl who chooses cuddle parties or group contact activities. Maybe you're not, either. So what have I learned about love?

I learned from science and my visions that my underlying storyline got in my way and caused me to be closed and suspicious, judgmental and defensive. And that's where I started. Over and over again in meditation, I went back to the end point of that story from my vision, the moment on the beach, and replaced the narrative, bit by bit, that accompanied the visuals. I created a monologue that focused on the beauty of the ocean rather than the rage and anger I felt. I reframed the burning in my lungs as the growing potency of my spirit about to burst forth. I recognized that no matter what *I* did, *he'd* never be any bigger than what he was, and that was not mine to fix. This process, over time, seemed to take the edge off my thoughts each time I thought about love, safety, and risk. I was no longer charged and in fight-or-flight mode when things inside of my relationships went wrong. This meditational script rehearsal seemed to give me more room in my daily life for forgiveness. I was judging less as my need to defend myself against phantoms disappeared. I rewrote a fantasy story that was underneath it all, regardless of whether the story itself was true. I was healing and opening my heart through the neuroplastic entrainment of my mind.

This was the first step in my ability to remain more grounded within relationships, and this led to an avalanche of realizations regarding how I functioned throughout my entire life. As I rescripted my stories and patterns, I also changed my diet slowly over time to fit more with what my mind wanted and less with what my limbic cravings dictated. And now, with a history of a cleaner diet, I can tell instantly that my mood gets compromised when I eat poorly. Regulation and restoration are much easier to engage with now.

Where there is one big story for each of us, there may be many more, smaller stories thematically similar. And the rewriting process is a lifelong practice of refinement. This is why I say I'm still learning about how to love. As the PFC gets highly activated in this focused rescripting, it strengthens itself and helps to prune back the neural maps dedicated to unwarranted fear responses. It takes advantage of our neurons' "use it or lose it" structure, and serves our greatest good. Without your brain in prime shape, you might continue to walk by the person in need, favoring your own convenience. You might continue to harbor grudges from twenty years ago. You might continue to feel secret vindication when your enemies fail. You might find reward in watching those who have hurt you finally get punished. You might use "an eye for an eye" as your lens on the world. Story by story, we can reframe and restructure so that the mind exercises itself into a more robust dynamic to maintain our spiritual desires—to be the best humans we can be.

Regardless of where you are with your own ability to love unconditionally, to dive fully into the depths of your fears, or to open to the world around you, you can still benefit from bringing diet, daily exercises, and mind into alignment and reworking your limiting stories. This will support your ability to learn how to love more deeply.

· · · · · · · · · · · ·

DISCOVERY JOURNAL **embracing love, version two**

Note one of your stories or memories that really seem to get in your way when it comes to offering or receiving love, one of those stories that pops up over and over each time you think you are done with it.

Maybe that's your story of not being enough, or the memory of the time you were embarrassed publicly so that now you shy away from things you love in hopes of saving face. Write down the details of that story as though you were telling it to someone who didn't know you. Label this as Version 1. Now, rewrite the story again labeling it as Version 2. This time, create new details that weren't there before. This will give a new perspective to the same event. For example, if you describe looking into the person's angry face in Version 1, add in a statement in Version 2 that feels true and realistic—for example, "As I stared at her angry face I wondered what would be different if we could have remembered the good times."

You are not looking to erase the story, but rather to add new perspectives into the old recall. In this way you can actively begin to put little breaks in the sticky context, opening it up so you can relate differently to it. After you've done this exercise, you can revisit Version 2 in meditations or in moments of pondering throughout your day to reinforce the new context. Notice over the next few weeks what might change about this memory or the effect it has in your current situation.

HEART, HEAD . . . AND FACE?

Just as we engage heart and head in our experience of love, we also engage the rest of our body, including our face and eyes. I've learned about love by looking at the faces of those who easily expressed love and those who easily expressed disgust, disdain, and stress. Imagine you are alone and in a foreign country where you don't speak the language. You need to find a safe place to stay for the evening. There are two locals sitting near you, both of them alone. One of them has a deeply furrowed brow, his eyebrows pinched together. He has frown lines worn into his face, and his lip curls up unconsciously with a small snarl. The other man has a relaxed mouth whose lips curl upwards at the corners. He's showing some teeth in a relaxed manner as he reads. His eyes look up occasionally from his book and he looks around, increasing his smile each time he inspects his environment. Which man are you more likely to approach? Most of us would choose the man who looks less stoic. Why?

There is much unspoken communication in our facial expressions that conveys a sense of safety, inclusion, and the opportunity to be acknowledged. As you read the description of the two men you might have even felt the muscles in your own face contract a bit as you imagined the man with the furrowed brow and snarl. Can you feel what your face wants to do when you simply think of that expression of disgust? I was never someone who could mask my emotions well, never able to feign a bright smile when I was sad or hide a snarl when I was outraged. Everything seemed to be written all over my face. Our face can be a barometer for what's going on in both the heart and the head.

Our facial muscles, unlike most of the other muscles in our body, communicate directly with the brainstem—our most primitive and reptilian control center. It makes perfect sense if you think of a baby who needs to learn to read the world through very limited experiences, beginning first with just the sounds of his parents' and family's voices, the warmth of their touch, and their big faces staring right at him. A baby needs to quickly be able to categorize and understand what a real smile is and what a furrowed and tense brow means. Identifying safe faces is a skill we learn early on which helps us drop our guard when we're safe, and become hypervigilant when we're in danger. It's a prime means of communicating how we feel about ourselves and the world around us.

Our reptilian response relies on our ability to distinguish safety or danger on another's face. Our ability to also make these expressions is as important as our ability to read them. In fact, the two are more linked then we ever suspected. Remember, with discoveries around the mirror neuron effect, we now understand that witnessing someone else's genuine smile sparks a neural map in my brain that maps to my own experience of smiling.[6] And what does this have to do with love and fear, head and heart? To experience love we need to be able to recognize it, give it, receive it, and embody it. To embody it we need to feel it. To feel it we need the impulses and messages to be clear in both the body and mind. If we can tap into our most primal center and relax it, then we can embody love more easily. Genuine smiles are both easier to recognize and cultivate when our primal self feels safe and can signal the face to convey that. In my vision with The Mother it was the man's angry eyes and an enraged face that anchored in my experience of danger. Try this exercise when the opportunity arises. Try bringing up a genuine smile when everyone around you is disgusted and clearly showing it. It will be more difficult as their facial expressions will create an influence on your own emotions.

When we are around those with loving expressions on their faces, we might be more inclined to feel or experience a loving expression bubbling up inside. I remember seeing a video of myself when I was sixteen, standing away from the crowd at a family event. I hadn't realized I was being filmed. My body language was closed, with my arms folded protectively across my chest. My head was tilted, and the expression on my face was disdainful and smug. Instantly when seeing this video, I felt all of those emotions surface—and also realized my intellect and wit were a very weak invitation for connection when it was up against this radiant negativity. So when I want to feel love and compassion, I first have to notice my own face, body, and thoughts. If I can bring my face to neutral, and perhaps even smile, then I can instantly begin managing the emotions that seem to be reflected in my negative facial expression. Openness, forgiveness, and love can actually start with a genuine smile.

Here's a simple exercise to see how effective it really is: The next time you're in traffic, think of one of the warmest memories you have, one that makes you smile effortlessly. Hold that genuine smile on your face and see how much you've changed your mood—even though traffic hasn't changed at all. The union of body, mind, and spirit in our search for wholeness means that we have multiple ways to understand and navigate our world. We can calm or amplify the thoughts through the face; we can support the brain's ability to be compassionate through our diet; we can combat the body's disease through the mind. Each way in simply leads to the other. Using neurosculpting, we can learn to dance in union with the many parts of us crying out to be heard.

LEARNING HOW TO LOVE LEADS
TO HIGHER CONSCIOUSNESS

Learning about love has not been totally confined to the mechanisms of my brain, heart, and diet. There is a spiritual side to this journey as well, which helps me to learn each day how much more I can access and give love. For me, this spiritual side involves learning more about consciousness. What exactly is consciousness? I can only offer my definition here. Consciousness is my ability to create perceptions of the various sensory stimuli I experience in my body and in my world through my skin, eyes, nose, ears, mouth, gut, and any other way in which I detect an experience. Without consciousness I may still experience sensory stimulus, but I'd have no ability to create a *perception* around that event. I'd have no ability to determine if that were good or bad, desirable or aversive. Consciousness is the end voice of all the percolations of my sensory and autonomic self. Sometimes my consciousness about an experience happens long after the sensory information was received, and sometimes my perceptions can form instantly. Consciousness involves my higher-order thought processes, and that evolved PFC. Without the PFC and neocortex, I may not have any perceptions at all, like someone in such a vegetative state as to have autonomic reflexes but nothing more.

If I believe I am a conscious being, here to express my connection to a higher source, then perhaps I have to believe the same about others. If I'm looking to others to reflect that nature, then I must assume they are conscious beings with a similar intention. But where does this idea of consciousness end? Are animals conscious? Are plants, without a cortex, conscious? What about minerals? This is a tremendous topic that I doubt will ever be closed. I have found that if I assume each thing I interact with has some level of consciousness, then I tend to treat that interaction with more attention, reverence, and respect than if I assumed otherwise. This assumption supports my ideas around being the best human I can be. Love and evolution rely on my perceptions, and my perceptions rely on my sense of consciousness. The more I view others as conscious beings, the more I have to look upon the world with a greater capacity for love.

How can consciousness help us break free from limiting and reactionary patterns that hold us back from love? How can consciousness open us to more reverence? Perhaps plants have an answer.

. . . .

PUTTING IT ALL TOGETHER cultivating love

This chapter touched upon some very loaded topics that can show up for us throughout our lives. That's a lot to take in, and it's not required that any of us arrive at a place of total forgiveness and unconditional love simply by reading this section. However, there are ripe opportunities in this chapter to open doors of lifelong learning and growth. To make the most of this journey through fear, love, and forgiveness you can start by revisiting the opening section on judgment and noting the ways in which we easily judge each other. Try writing in the margins or in your journal the ways in which you judge others, except be sure to use the past tense in each statement. For example:

- I **was** judgmental of my friend's religious beliefs.
- I **used to** judge my neighbors based on their political affiliations.
- I **judged** my spouse's extracurricular activities as an excuse to spend time away from me.

You don't have to do much more than list these. The important part of this new integration is that you see and hear in your mind the past tense of this practice. There's a great power in speaking and writing something into our own reality.

To help make the most out of the section titled "Neural Mechanisms of Love" I recommend rereading the studies mentioned. They focus on the power of love to mitigate anxiety and stress. You can begin to reflect upon your own experiences of feeling relaxed and wonderful during times of safety, support, and love. Try noting some details about how you remember your body felt during those times. Maybe you had a sense of calm, or your cheeks were flushed. Perhaps you noticed you smiled more. Take some time here to remember those body states with your eyes closed.

To make this material even more alive for you, consider the exercise you did in the forgiveness section where you noted some key events that have gripped you and kept you stuck in judgment. If you'd like to challenge yourself even more to embody this information you can choose to make amends to those individuals you noted you needed to forgive. You can do this in a visual exercise where you imagine yourself saying what you need to say, or you can choose to do this in real time if that's the right approach for you. Integrating means taking content and words off the page and into a practice. Decide how you want to practice forgiveness as you embody this information.

As you absorb all of this more deeply you can begin changing your body behavior as well. It takes a daily intentional practice to change the muscle patterning we carry in our faces. To begin, take some time to look at yourself in the mirror. This is best done when you're alone. Try having a handheld mirror with you for a little while during a day in which you are doing normal activities. During random times throughout an activity, just glance at the expression on your face quickly without getting stuck in examining your reflection. Notice if your predominant facial expression has a pinched brow or a gentle smile. This will give you a good sense of how others see you during your normal routine. Some of us might be surprised to note how often our facial expressions indicate that something is bothering us.

My husband mirrors me beautifully and often makes me laugh. At times when I'm emphatically trying to get my point across, he'll look at me and raise his eyebrows as high as they can go in a ridiculous manner. At first, I didn't know what he was doing. Now I know each time he does that, it's because he's mirroring me. A few times I've even quickly caught my face in the mirror and noticed how it added an extra charge to what I was saying, even though I didn't mean it in that manner. The mirror exercise can be quite revealing.

To integrate some of this further, you could practice changing your facial expressions in the car, at work, shopping, and even while you are thinking negatively about someone. You can begin to repattern the very muscles that communicate most to your brain about your safety and well-being. I wonder how much you could let go of or forgive if you cultivated a real heartfelt smile each time you were poised to remember someone in their worst light.

8

the nature of consciousness:
what a plant told me

Plants are the young of the world,
vessels of health and vigor;
but they grope ever upward towards consciousness;
the trees are imperfect men, and seem to bemoan
their imprisonment, rooted in the ground.

RALPH WALDO EMERSON

We've journeyed quite a ways together. So far we've discussed the power of neuroplasticity in the mind's functioning, and its relationship to the body state. We've noted the ways in which mental entrainment can work for or against us in creating important guiding patterns in our lives. We've noted that these patterns can be loaded with a fear charge or the charge of discovery. We've looked at ways in which our thoughts influence the way we interact with the world and how they cultivate things like free will, resilience, hope, judgment, forgiveness, and love. And all of these thought and body patterns choreograph our ability to heal our trauma, rewrite our beliefs, and experience life with more awareness.

We've learned that if we step out of the limitation of our fear-based limbic mode we can harness more of the creative and empathic nature of the PFC. We've seen that when we increase our empathy we can move ourselves into modes of forgiveness. It's possible to see others in a different light, discover aspects and perspectives we didn't know were there, and increase the depth and breadth of our view of the world.

Let's take an even more fantastical journey now where we consider the far end of the spectrum of empathy and discovery. Neurosculpting has armed me with a set of tools to recognize and step beyond the veils of my stories and into a space of infinite possibility. I'm not there in every moment, but the more I sculpt, the easier it is to get there.

Imagine what would be possible for you if you could slide your stories aside and peek out from behind all of them to witness the magic that was in front of you. How astounded would you be to learn the way in which you've related to the world up to now were as though you wore sunglasses in the dark? There is a world of vibrant colors far beyond what we expect to see once we become adept at putting aside our stories and thoughts for a little while.

Interestingly, neurosculpting has led me into endeavors that some others call the psychic realm. But before we get into a charged conversation about what it means to be psychic, I want to tell you what I mean when I use that term. Although it may seem magical, I don't use the term to imply any sort of magic or even special skill. Psychic, for me, means having cultivated a neurosculpting practice that helps me identify, remember, and step away from my constructed stories so that I open my vision to what's directly in front of me. And sometimes, what's in front of me is far more than I might have seen through my limiting beliefs. I use neurosculpting in a very pragmatic sense. I liken it to wiping glasses clean to clear one's vision.

Think about this example. If I asked an elderly man with poor eyesight to describe a face he looked upon, he might recognize a pair of eyes and their color, a nose, and a mouth. For his visual capability, he'd be correct. If I asked someone with perfect vision to describe the same face, they might agree with the man's descriptions and add in a description of some freckles and moles, or even a small scar. The person with perfect vision is also correct in describing the face based on visual capability, yet to the older man, this person may be seeing things that are "invisible."

Now what if I asked a tetrachromat to describe the face? This is someone who has four different types of cones in their eyes versus the normal three and can see up to one hundred million colors for which we have no names. In 2010, neuroscientists at the University of Newcastle found the first identified tetrachromat, a woman.[1] She would describe the eyes very differently from anyone else asked. She would not be wrong, yet none of us could see what she saw. This is precisely how I view psychic phenomena—the ability, learned or innate, to see more of what's there due to a removal of story filters.

Let me give you another example of what at first may seem magical. This video is just one of many readily available on the Internet. The one I like to show is called "An Awareness Test" (https://www.youtube.com/watch?v=rxJnkTH6i_8) and it is a brief one-minute video of two teams playing an impromptu basketball game. The directions at the beginning instruct viewers to pay attention to how many times one team in particular passes the ball. In the middle of the game, a person in a gorilla suit comes out to center court and dances for a bit, and then exits.

Most people never see the gorilla when asked to describe the game, yet they are very focused on reporting how many times the one team passed the ball. I use this video in my trainings with law enforcement agencies to prove a point about selective blindness. At the end of the first viewing, I mention that I'm about to show a virtually identical video, only this time something completely unexpected happens. I show the very same video, and this time most of the audience instantly sees the gorilla and begins to chuckle.

To me, this is exactly the same principle as my version of psychic awareness. What storyline or filter was the audience looking through the first time, which literally blinded their conscious mind to what their vision picked up? What new storyline was engaged for them to then see what was directly in front of them the next time? It appears magical that one could be so certain there was nothing there. But then, moments later, be so certain there is a person in a gorilla suit. The only difference was the change of story, or filter, through which the audience viewed the world.

Dr. Norman Katz, who was influential in creating medical hypno-therapy in the latter half of the last century, likes to refer to these lenses as "trances." Where I ask you to notice what story is your filter, he'd ask you what trance you're in. *This* is my experience of psychic awareness. Neurosculpting away my limiting stories has enabled me to view more than what I saw before. I am certainly not asking you to believe in psychic ability, nor am I interested in proving the existence of psychic ability. What I am interested in is sharing with you some phenomenal experiments I participated in which caused me to question and let go of even more of my outdated stories.

WHAT A PLANT SHOWED ME

I was invited into the engineering research laboratory at the University of Colorado–Boulder for various experiments with plants. One of the leading questions in the experiments was: are plants conscious? Remember that earlier I gave you my definition of consciousness: the ability to make a *perception* about a stimulus. While we can't measure if a plant makes a perception, we can measure the responses plants have to certain stimuli, and then researchers can make interpretations from there. I'm sharing what happened in that lab for two reasons: it is fascinating to learn about the idea of plant conscious-ness, and it's even more fascinating to me to learn about how much is possible if we neurosculpt away our limitations and intentionally create storylines that open doors of our own heightened perception. This might be more esoteric than some of the content of the book thus far, but it falls farther along the spectrum of the potential of neurosculpting. It helped me enfold my physical reality into the importance of my spiritual reality. It was through these experiments that my own ideas around consciousness expanded and I gained a greater reverence for all of life. After these experiments, I was never able to view my environment the same way again.

In the summer of 2012, Professor Garret Moddel, head of the Depart-ment of Electrical, Computer, and Energy Engineering, contacted me.

He is an extremely sweet and unassuming man whose keen interest in quantum engineering and psi phenomena led to his experiments with plant consciousness research using *Iresine* and *Dracaena* plants. He introduced me to his Brazilian researcher, Luiz Estavao, who was finishing up his doctorate. Luiz is a very jovial and effusive personality whose culture and wonderful accent seemed to amplify his excitement for the plants he worked with. It struck me that he was not afraid to use the language of emotions when referring to the plants he so clearly enjoyed having a relationship with. He spoke about them affectionately and told me he'd grown very fond of them over the months of research.

When I arrived at the university, Luiz greeted me with a customary kiss on both cheeks. This was not at all the greeting I expected from an engineer in the lab. He excitedly took me into the very sterile-looking engineering building, and we wandered through a maze of dimly lit hallways en route to the lab. There was more equipment than there was room, and the air smelled mechanical and stale. The decor was mostly wires, machines, outlets, hard metal surfaces, cinderblock walls, and muted gray colors. It felt as though I were entering a futuristic cave. I don't think there was a soft surface in the space, which caused the bright green plants near the window to stand out even more than they might have otherwise. They were a vibrant splash of life and color next to one of the few natural sources of light in the lab. They were so out of place amidst the subtle buzz of technology and jagged shapes, yet they, too, were hooked up to machines.

Luiz explained to me that the plants were wired to a galvanic skin-response machine, like a lie-detector device, which would measure fluctuations in their moisture levels. His relationship to and affinity for the plants was at the forefront of each action as I watched him gently reset the insertion points, being careful not to stab the plant roots unnecessarily. He even told me that the plants didn't like it when he poked them too many times or too harshly.

The room was separately hooked up to a random events generator (REG) to measure changes in the room. In a way, it's a type of electronic coin flipper, only instead of flipping coins, it generates a random output occurrence of either 1s or 0s. The REGs, although still used for speculative rather than empirical data, seem to be highly affected by shifts in consciousness of the environment. Basically, changes in the conscious interactions in the room will create disturbances in the normal randomized patterns of output. This serves as a speculative marker of an environmental shift of consciousness.

Both the REG and the galvanic skin-response machines sent signals to the computer screen. The plants generated unique sine wave outputs, clearly noting one frequency for the *Iresine* and a different one for the *Dracaena,* like handwriting samples. It was fascinating to look at the two unique signatures.

Luiz showed me other printouts of their signatures as they fluctuated with different events of the day: their signatures during that season's devastating forest fires; the activity when one very abrasive researcher often walked in the lab; their signatures when they were wrapped in aluminum foil, etc. More amazingly, the REG readings correlated to the sine wave fluctuations in the plants in these cases. Clearly the plants' output varied for each event in its own unique way. Could this be interpreted as the plants' preferences for certain situations?

The first experiment Luiz asked me to do had little to do with neurosculpting but was so profound that it opened the door to the rest of what we did. I was asked to play music for the plants, so I chose to play my Hang drum. This is a very unique drum, which creates a melodic and resonant sound so beautiful that I've never heard anything like it. It looks like a space ship, is made of metal, and resonates different notes based on various depressions in the surface. I chose my favorite drum for this experiment, as I've seen this drum cause people to slip happily and instantly into reverie and joy. It is the same drum I played for a woman on her deathbed as she transitioned with a smile and steady heart rate.

As I hit the first note, Luiz became intrigued as the unique and independent sine waves of each plant rapidly converged on the computer screen. For the duration of my ten or fifteen minutes of playing, the plants' output mapped synchronistically as though they had one mirrored signature. Luiz had never seen them do that before. This lasted until the point at which I began my musical outro, when they slowly began reestablishing their own original signatures.

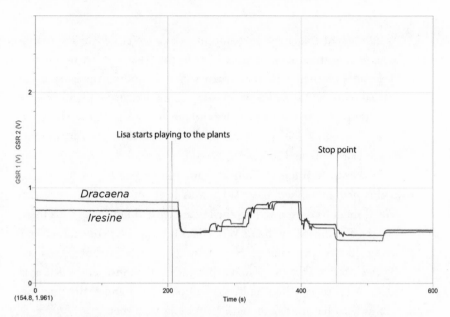

Peaks and valleys correlate synchronistically. The black line—the output of the *Iresine*—responds to the sound of the music a fraction of a second before the output of the *Dracaena*—the gray line.

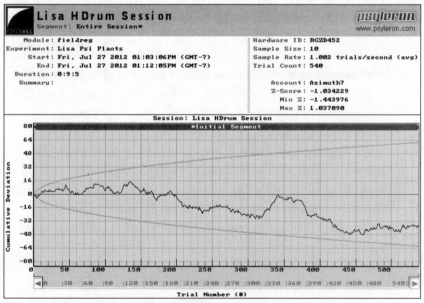

Random Events Generator (REG) output reflecting the laboratory environment during the plant experiment.

157

Luiz noted that in the ten-minute session pictured in the graphs there were statistical deviations even in the REG, which meant that likely all the energy in that space suffered modifications from the normal pattern. "The most interesting thing is that the plants reacted *after* you played to them (there was no precognition), but the Random Event Generator 'felt' the intentions and started to react before you played to the plants (200 sec)."

What was it about the music that caused these plants to sync up in this choreographed way? What was it about this experience that caused them to do something the researcher had not seen in his many months of monitoring them? What does it mean when one intentional action, like playing music, causes a unified effect in those experiencing the music? Were the plants experiencing the music and shifting in relationship to it? This result was so unexpected and intriguing that Luiz asked what more I thought I could do with them.

I suggested that I go into some neurosculpting meditations and "read" Luiz. This meant that I would look at Luiz from a very neutral space, doing my best to push aside any stories I had about me, him, or our environment, and see what thoughts about him came to mind. This state of awareness required me to shut down my fight-flight-or-freeze reactions, calm my nervous system, and access an experience of being something more than that which I understand. It required that I step out of my left prefrontal analysis and into my right prefrontal predisposition for insight and awe. This state required my highest levels of neurosculpting practice.

We wanted to see if the plants would shift their output in relationship to the way I shifted my own. Could they register and respond to someone in stress and someone in expanded ease? Would they even notice? He hooked the plants and room up to his equipment to see if there would be any fluctuations as the plants shared space with us during this activity. What happened was astounding.

I began my neurosculpting meditations to clear my thoughts and expectations, to ground myself into an ease of body and relaxation of limbic thoughts. I cleared away any stories that might inhibit my ability to be neutral or cause me to suspect, judge, or surmise. I prepared myself to be in a novel space of curiosity and observation. I began to read Luiz, describing the images that seemed to come at random. It was not my job to interpret anything, as that would put me into a cognitive space of trying to make sense of the situation. Instead, I stayed in curiosity and simply narrated the scenes that unfolded with no expectation.

My eyes were closed, so I could have no visual cues from Luiz as to the accuracy or relevance of the images. This reading was just like many I've done in which I feel like a storyteller. There were no sensational or earth-shattering images, no discussions of any past life relationships with Cleopatra or other such stereotypical depictions of this sort of experience. Yet at one point during the course of my reading, the crystal-clear image of the *Iresine* plant jumped into my mind's eye and interrupted my reading. It literally brought the other images to a halt. I perceived it told me it had urgent information to give Luiz, and it proceeded to tell me a message I was to communicate to him.

I was giggling by this time, communicating to Luiz that as ridiculous as it sounded, the plant interrupted my reading and needed him to know something. After I communicated this message, I continued with the images that came and finished the reading. The *Dracaena* remained quiet and outside of my awareness throughout the reading.

Luiz had his eyes open during the reading, diligently taking notes, monitoring the plants' wave output, the REG, and the audio equipment recording the session. He had a funny look on his face when I opened my eyes at the end of the experience, the kind of look when a child believes he saw Santa Claus. He was very excited to show me that at precisely the time I reported being interrupted by the *Iresine,* that very plant's sine wave output spiked considerably during the experience and maintained an elevated spike during the time in which I reported it was communicating with me. The *Dracaena* had no spike in output.

What was happening for the plant that caused such a distinct and timely spike? Was the plant communicating with me as my narrative suggested? Was all of this just a series of random serendipity? Of course, to an empirical scientist, this data might not mean what I interpreted it to mean. Nevertheless, I had multiple direct experiences in which the plant life in the room seemed to shift and respond in direct relationship to my own limbic-state modulations, as did the REG's output. Whatever the numbers and outputs mean, one thing was clear: all devices and beings in the room fluctuated in synchrony throughout our time together. To me, this was an experience in a form of consciousness.

In the context of neurosculpting, this experience could only happen because I've spent many years practicing a method that has strengthened my ability to quiet my limiting prediction scripts, and focus my awareness on cultivating the curiosity of the PFC.

Imagine how much more you could perceive when you quiet your fear-based mind as you've learned throughout the book. You could be open to the vast expanse of your PFC's ability to entertain new situations with an inquisitive nature rather than a threat defense. The more you use your PFC to enhance your sense of focused awareness, the more you heighten your neuroplasticity and begin to turn those experiences into stored patterns that can be built upon. In this state of focused attention and heightened neuroplasticity, we have the ability to open our perceptions in order to recognize interesting relationships with others and our environment we might not normally know are there. It's similar to seeing the gorilla in the video after swearing nothing was there just moments before. As I stood in the lab with Luiz, I began noticing something uniquely synchronistic between my own energy and the energies of the plants. While we'll never know what the experience was like for the plants, my ability to step out of my own scripts and into a state of focused and open attention caused my spirit to feel that it was a part of something greater, something unnamable. I didn't expect to have a spiritual experience in an engineering lab, but that's precisely what happened.

Paradoxically, doing this sort of spiritual work seemed to be that much stronger as science participated in the event. Science yielded its own information about a very intangible experience. Data, numbers, machines, observers, calculations, controls, historical information, and measurable moments wove seamlessly with emotional opening, spiritual expansion, and energetic communication. For me, these experiments are examples of neurosculpting in the world, examples of how the empirical can hold space for the intangible. It was an example of how stepping outside of expectations and into simple observation on both the scientist's part and my own caused both of us to have a profound experience—which neither of us expected. The experiment opened up a nonjudgmental two-way dialogue between all that is unseen and all that is measurable. I believe both of us were humbled in realizing that neither of us had a concrete way in which to explain the synchronistic and magical results of the experiments.

What if you were to stop hiding behind all you think you know? What more could you notice about the wonders of life? Maybe you'd see the gorilla standing in front of you this whole time. You might hear the same old conversation with new ears and realize you've missed a lot in your relationships. You could recognize aspects of loved ones you had been blind to. Perhaps in learning more about what's going on around you, you might even increase your sense of wonder for the great mysteries of life that are easily disguised in the mundane. I can assure you, I'll never look at a plant the same way again. This sense of prefrontal focused attention can remind us of our childlike curiosity. What if in your die-hard grip of data and proof, you entertained the idea that it's only proof based on your limited knowledge up to now? What if you realized the more you know, the more there is to know and experience? This is how we challenge ourselves to step out of judgment.

Let's assume you don't have a science research lab at your disposal, and you want to start cultivating this openness and sense of wonder right now. You can begin in this very moment with this next exercise to recognize that what you think you know about how the world truly is may only be a fraction of the total picture.

• • • • • • • • • • • •

DISCOVERY JOURNAL cultivating wonder

Note some of the things you believed whole-heartedly when you were younger based on the "facts" of the time but that are no longer true. An example might be that brain cells can't be regenerated, only to find out later they can, or that smoking while pregnant was safe. If you've grown up like me, then it might be a "fact" like there is nothing smaller than an atom. For this exercise, you might need to think back to your childhood and the facts of the time in which you grew up. After each so-called fact, note if you met the changing reality with novelty and curiosity or with staunch resistance. End this exercise with this question prompt: "What if I could gracefully accept today's knowledge and balance that with the knowing that it might change tomorrow?"

. . . .

PUTTING IT ALL TOGETHER **cultivating nonjudgment**

This chapter was all about opening yourself to new experiences and information and stepping into a sense of wonder and curiosity. You can experiment in your own life with getting your logical mind and your experiential mind to speak to each other in a way that causes each to support the other. Try entertaining these few questions to jump-start your exploration into wonderment by pretending you are a tourist in your hometown:

- What new restaurants do you notice?
- What hobbies do you seek out?
- What new parks do you find?
- What new neighbors can you meet?
- What new local attractions can you visit?
- What can you learn about the history of your town?

You might begin to realize that when you view your day-to-day world with inquiry and wonder, you begin to expand your perceptions. Where in your own life can you begin to soften a hard stance to make room for yourself to be expanded and surprised?

To help integrate the discussion on consciousness, you can begin by paying attention to the plants around your house, maybe even choosing half of them to talk to each day in a calm and happy voice to notice if they seem to be more vibrant over time, or different from the ones you don't pay attention to.

To embody this information further it's helpful to hear yourself talk about these concepts. Begin by writing down the serendipitous occurrences in your life each week, noticing that with or without a scientific explanation, they still happen. Then encourage some dinner conversation with family or friends to discuss everyone's experience or perceptions of serendipity. There's no need to go into a place of proof or disproof, as this is just an exercise in conversing about the ideas rather than choosing a stance. You might even find that as you begin to pay attention and bring this idea into your awareness that it seems to happen more and more. If you can stay in wonderment, these moments can become rich conversations rather than debates. The benefit is that through engaged dialogue you can end up discovering more about your own relationship to these ideas. Through this sort of inquiry we get to refine our own thoughts and deepen our understanding of concepts we might not have thought about before. In this way, we expand our own perceptions and approach life in a prefrontal disposition of curiosity and enhanced learning.

9

judgment

People hasten to judge
in order not to be judged themselves.

ALBERT CAMUS, *The Fall*

The pain was great, a lifetime of trying to please, an eternity of tiptoe-ing around disapproving glances. There was fear: do not leave me alone with him as he will punish me, callously. He uses sharp edges, barbed words, and grand gestures of intimidating power. Mother, please do not leave him alone with me. But The Mother could only do what her compassion dictated, and so she said I must be alone with him.

I had wondered if I should confront him to tell him of all the pain he inflicts. But I'd only be attached to his response, hoping for a sign that he'd heard me. And I already knew that hoping for validation only brought me disappointment. No, this was not the way. My healing could only come from me. So I conceded, as though I had a choice, and let The Mother take me to the Arena.

It sprawled across the universe, open to the stars and the com-ings and goings of galactic winds. It served as a bazaar that provided goods and services for clamoring hordes of souls en route to what was next. How would I find him in the public sea of wisps and shadows?

I walked through phantoms and oases, little villages and darkened paths. I approached the center of the Arena, and there he was, wait-ing with purpose. Yet I surprised him with my presence. The din died down, and all souls retreated to the farthest curves of the Arena to watch from a distance, as though our stepping into the center signified a commencement. Would this be a spectacle? Could I hold back the rage that provoked my screams and fists? The Mother's black wave rumbled underneath my bones, and she reminded me about the pause that comes with breath.

I breathed in deeply, relaxing into expansion, vaguely detecting the smell of confusion and remorse. And suddenly I was outside of my fear, anger, and sadness. I was bigger, spreading myself like a vibrantly colored light. I looked upon him to see his essence do the same until we radiated brightly next to each other and blinded the spectators with our size. I saw that he was not that form that caused me so much pain—and that I was not that form that was steeped in fear. We were so much more than that, here in this Arena.

How could I have been blind to this before? How could my own stories have made us both so dim? From this vibrant expansion I bowed to his brightness, and he to mine. Pieces of my own color streamed back to me as they separated and released from his space, spiraling out in strands. Deeply embedded threads uncoiled from my depths and returned back to him. My spaces were my own again, both empty and full.

It was over. The contract was complete. We learned what we needed to learn from each other in this powerful relationship, and it was time to move on. I bowed and the Arena was no more.

The Mother told me I might never see a time in my current lifetime when our real-time bodies caught up to this new relationship. We might never come to acknowledge to the other the brightness we saw. I might never communicate with him again through the limiting filters of our existence. But I knew that everything was changed, healed, and we'd joke about it again when our bodies were just memories.

WHAT IS JUDGMENT?

There are ways in which judgment serves to make us better, more expansive individuals. After all, we are always judging something. For example, you may judge that eating healthy foods is a better way to live. That judgment can work for your greatest good, as it serves your well-being and does not harm others. However, when that judgment falls too far to one side of the spectrum, it can be distorted into a condemnation of people who do not care about a healthy diet. We are dealing with a very subjective topic, and each one of us must decide for his or herself where we draw the line to determine whether our judgmental nature is serving us or limiting us.

I believe that judgment is when I have a story or script that I use as a lens for my outlook, behaviors, and patterns. If that story supports my well-being and isn't harmful to others, then it becomes a tool I can use to help me make choices that are in my best interest. If that story is one that limits me, contracts me, or causes my limbic system to become active, then I will look through that lens in a fight-flight-or-freeze manner or an "us and them" mentality. When I have a story like that, then my limbic response will be to prove or defend my stance. When I use judgment this way I may even find myself attacking others with the actions or words of disapproval, condemnation, and even righteousness.

This is judgment turned outward and thrown onto others. This is when judgment bites us hard and does nothing to create a "toward" response between people or communities. It becomes a line in the sand we hide behind, and an arbitrary territory we vehemently defend. With extreme judgment at the helm, we are no different than Don Quixote chasing phantoms and battling windmills. To me, judgment turned outward and projected is simply a proclamation of being completely outside one's comfort zone or not in touch with one's own power.

Judgment is the cornerstone of a divide, and at its most harmful, it causes individuals to create alliances and adversaries. "Us and them" is a fundamental survival mechanism that might come in handy for self-preservation in crisis, but it does little to foster expansion, communication, empathy, compassion, or creative solutions for the betterment of all.

I was a very judgmental person, latching on to stories about others to make my own stories seem better or morally correct. Why do we need to do this? Do we need to do this when we are in our own power, confident and sure of our own motivations? I don't think so. When The Mother offered me my experience in the Arena, I realized that the moment I stepped into my own power, I no longer needed to judge. I didn't have to tiptoe anymore, seeking to please those who'd never approve of my actions. I no longer needed to be argumentative if someone disagreed with my stance. I could choose to keep my mouth shut when I heard others I disagreed with fighting to prove their cases.

When I am comfortable with my inner stories, I don't need to chase endless trails of proof. When we step out of judgment, we can let go of the *need* to be heard and simply know that we hear ourselves. We can drop the urgency around getting the other person to understand us, because the truth is that they might never get there. As long as we keep our own sense of satisfaction or self-worth tied to the other person's acceptance or approval of our ideas, we will always be limited and never free. We may always seek refuge and safety behind our limiting stories, sticking to them even at the expense of our own well-being. Recognizing and moving beyond our judgmental nature is part of the neurosculpting process in which we identify which judgment scripts no longer serve us, and use our own gifts of focused attention and plasticity to create better scripts. Stepping outside of judgment as much as possible enables me to see others in a greater light, and it cultivates a compassion for the stories they may be using to limit themselves.

Not only does staunch judgment cause us to take stances and foster an "us and them" mentality, it can spiral into unwarranted attacks, antagonism, bigotry, racism, and even violence. And all of this is a defense of our attachment to our own constructed thoughts. None of us is immune from having wielded our judgment against someone or something, and each of us has the ability to temper that en route to healing and living from a place of wholeness. My vision showed me that the stance and judgment I felt for the man in the Arena only kept me small, and once I dropped it I expanded into a bigger version of myself. How much more vibrant could you be if you dropped your energy-consuming judgments?

• • • • • • • • • • • •

i just can't help myself

Note some inflammatory times in which you were compelled beyond control to argue about your point of view with someone you knew beyond a doubt would never concede your opinion. After noting each of these, write this question prompt and see if you can answer honestly: "Even though I knew the other person would never accept my point of view, I engaged in the argument anyway because . . . "

In this exercise, did you judge someone else's morals? Did you judge your own? Were you feeling as though they judged you? Did any of that create the outcome that makes your heart feel warm, your body relaxed, and your mind open to the wonderful potential of your life? Maybe you even remember how your body felt during the argument or debate. Were you amped up on adrenaline? Was your heart racing, your voice louder or quivery? Were you sweating? Did you clench your jaw or get a lump in your throat? Maybe you even felt all of that again as you wrote about those times.

JUDGMENT IS SYMPATHETIC, BUT NOT IN THE WAY YOU THINK

It might be clear to you that during times in which we're judging others or are being judged by others, we are not in our body's preferred healing space of parasympathetic response. We're not in homeostasis or restoration where our breathing is deep and slow, or our muscles are relaxed and loose. We're likely not in a place of low heart rate and prime nutritional absorption. We're probably in engagement, mobility, and fight-flight-or-freeze mode where we are preparing to protect and defend our beliefs, or to battle for a cause. And unless we're actually going into battle, why are we doing this to ourselves?

The kind of judgment that causes this sort of response can only help us train the limbic system and inhibit our abilities to access all of those higher human traits that can make us the best people we can be. If your neighbor isn't harming anyone, what good does it serve your body, your being, and your life to be angry or irritated, therefore engaging a limbic existence? This is an over-investment in things beyond your control that keeps you engaged in areas of your life that disempower you. It's simple. Energy and attention spent in areas outside of your control just keep you feeling that life *is* outside of your control! In these cases it's important to rewrite that defense pattern and begin to take our own power back.

There's an entire field of research now called social cognitive neuroscience in which the prefrontal cortex is associated with our social existence and interactions. In this current field of study, there are two systems we can think about when trying to understand our social experiences: the reflexive system and the reflective system.[1] The reflexive system is what it sounds like: a quick reflex. Some neuroscientists believe it comprises some key limbic structures, one being the amygdala. This system is involved in quickly analyzing a social situation that meets our existing underlying assumptions, judgments, and expectations, and seamlessly navigating that as an automated reflex. It's efficient and doesn't require much thought.

However, when we are met with social situations that do not meet our existing assumptions or expectations—our prediction scripts—we require a moment to pause for some other brain mechanisms to step in and navigate that discrepancy. This is known as the reflective system, in which we need time to reflect upon that which we're experiencing in order to make some executive decisions around it. Think about this scenario: Let's imagine that you go to the library often to read, research, or find quiet time. Over a very short period of time, you will have an expectation script that predicts what you should experience each time you go there. You expect to see books and computers. You expect to see people deep in quiet thought. You even expect for the smells and sounds to be similar.

But say one day you go to the library and instead of these familiar sights, you walk into a room of completely empty shelves, the smell of food cooking, and individuals in workout clothes stretching in the aisles. This situation does not meet your prediction script and will

cause you to pause and figure out what the nature of this new experience is. You might step back outside and reread the sign over the
door to validate that you are, in fact, at the library because suddenly
you question your certainty. You might look over your shoulder for
some hidden cameras, thinking you are on a reality show as you try to
grasp for a cause. You might even stop in your tracks with shock and
begin to ramble some statements of disbelief as you search for others
in shock with whom you can form an alliance. This is your reflective
system kicking in to negotiate the huge discrepancy in your reality
versus your prediction script. The reflective system is associated with
the activity of our PFC.[2] If we are met with social issues beyond our
comfort zone, then we have to spend valuable resources to pause
our subconscious reflexes and harness the power to evaluate them.
Many times, if we evaluate that a situation requires a lot of rescripting or too much navigating, we might still choose to default to our
reactionary response. What if we're not well-fed on the fuel the brain
needs during those times? What if we're exhausted and overworked?
What if we already have a predisposition to negativity and stress?
How well will we be able to press the pause button on our reflexive
system and move into reflection? Probably not very well. And what
do you think your limbic system will want to do with a script that
doesn't match its expectations when the PFC is too depleted to effec-
tively reflect upon it? You will likely take that situation and label it
as *error, wrong,* or *threat.*

In my opinion, this basis of brain behavior and this idea of
investing energy into the lives of others—over which we have no
control—becomes the root of the ugliest racism and prejudices we
have today. Are you understanding how easy it is to see someone else's
choices and lifestyle as a subconscious survival threat to your own if
you are not comfortable in your own power in the first place? As we are
faced with these perceived threats, our brain goes into a form of cross
talk, trying to negotiate all the potential risk factors and outcomes,
getting itself potentially stuck in a conflicted mess.

Many of us don't want to be judgmental because we know what it
feels like to be judged, yet we easily feel judgment arise all on its own.

Feeling judged can cause you to feel disempowered or unacknowledged. When your beliefs and choices about life are negated isn't it almost natural to get angry or frustrated? Being on the receiving end of judgment can also cause us to no longer feel kinship with the person judging. Suddenly, there is a divide, and this can feel like you are no longer "one of us." These feelings are the types of emotions that can result from threats to our prefrontal disposition, as they can spiral us quickly into a fight-or-flight response.

As intelligent humans, we're expected to rise above it, so we begin an inner struggle to control and regulate that judgmental behavior because many of us believe we should be better than that. Recent neuroscientific studies have shown that a part of the PFC called the anterior cingulate cortex steps in to try to regulate or arbitrate our inner conflict, particularly when it comes to judgment of others, as with prejudice.[3] If we need parts of our PFC to step in during times when judgment arises, and this part of the brain has the ability to make an executive decision that moves us out of a limbic reaction, then it stands to reason that identifying exercises to strengthen this ability may be helpful in this process. Neurosculpting becomes a way to remove the judgment filters we choose while simultaneously calming the limbic system so that the removal of those judgments can be graceful and long lasting. How amazing would it feel to be able to meet a completely unexpected safe situation with childlike wonder rather than with the feeling of inconvenience or threat?

If digging in deeply to our judgmental stances keeps us in a limbic loop, and we know exactly what a limbic lifestyle does to our health and emotional well-being, then doesn't it seem like maybe some of our stances are killing us slowly?

Where are you hiding behind your stances? Where can you soften some of them to give your brain a rest from its sympathetic arousal? Which stances can you identify as trivial so that your brain can take a break from negotiating irrelevant cross talk?

I remember a fabulous lesson I learned around this while trying to potty train my daughter. She was a very smart and articulate child, speaking full sentences very early on. I had no doubt that all I'd have to do was explain to her someday about the concept of the toilet and she'd get it quickly. As the two-year mark approached, friends and other mothers told me that I was missing the prime window to introduce the idea to her. They told me that if I didn't get her to use the toilet by that age, I'd be in for a huge problem. So though I hadn't been worried before, I began to feel a sense of urgency in starting her potty training. I did all the things I was told to do: read books, watched videos, introduced a potty for fun, then began to have her sit on it. She responded perfectly, easing my concern. And that's where it stopped. She didn't seem to go beyond loving the videos, talking about the concept, and reading the books. She was not applying the training. *Now* what was I going to do? I became judgmental regarding her development, my abilities as a mother, and her own sense of comparison to other toddlers. Each time I tried to get her to use the toilet, I felt a limbic response more and more quickly. My concerns were very much invested in a situation I had little control over: her desire to learn how to use the toilet. I viewed my own teaching skills as inadequate, looked at other potty-trained families with envy, and began to judge her by hearing myself refer to her as stubborn. Clearly, my judgments weren't helping me, or her. Her behavior was not meeting my prediction scripts of the effective and competent mother I once thought I was! We were both stressed.

Out of pure frustration and self-preservation, I dropped the battle completely and put her back in diapers at two-and-a-half years old. It didn't feel good for me to judge myself, or her, anymore. I began to feel better, have more patience, and move out of a limbic response. I was able to step back and look at the big picture with my prefrontal faculties. I told myself this: as most humans learn in their own way, she was sure to learn how to use the toilet *even* if I never taught her. I became sure of this as I couldn't think of one person I knew in my entire life who didn't know how to use the toilet! Surely, my daughter would not be the one person on Earth who failed at this permanently!

I thoroughly enjoyed the next six months of not fighting with her or carrying around multiple changes of clothes and towels in case of accidents. And then something miraculous happened. She wanted to go camping with me and was very excited about using those cool-looking gray things with doors. As only a child could see them, she viewed the port-a-potty as an intriguing place or a magical door. I told her those were only for people who regularly used the toilet. Her response was, "Okay, I'll use the toilet, then." That was the day *she* took off her diapers—and never once had an accident during the day or evening. My judgments about her abilities, my mothering skills, and her social development had been completely wrong. All she needed was to have a self-directed, enticing, and relevant goal in mind and make her own decision to attain it. I was clearly dangling all the wrong carrots!

Sometimes we don't even realize the source of our judgments or the fact that they are not relevant to the situation at all. How do you begin to know your battles?

• • • • • • • • • • • •

DISCOVERY JOURNAL choose your battles

List a few key times when you were stuck in a stance or judgment only to find a stalemate in which you had to completely yield and notice how events played out. Note how it felt in your mind and body to be rigid in that stance and how it felt when you gave it up. If it felt worse to give it up, note why. If it felt better, note why. Use this exercise to begin looking at each moment you are in a firm stance to better determine which ones you'd prefer to hold on to and which to give up.

It's easy for us to be overtaken in the heat of the moment, gripping firmly to the roller-coaster ride of our judgments. During these times I deepen my breath, step away from the stance, and do something unrelated like listen to music, walk, or some other enjoyable activity, and then I do some neurosculpting meditations around the topic.

. . . .

PUTTING IT ALL TOGETHER cultivating curiosity

As you consider this idea of judgment, you can create a deeper relationship with this content by going back through this chapter and using the margins to answer some of the rhetorical questions in the text. You see, they are not meant to be rhetorical! Taking the time to answer some of these questions strengthens your own inquiry and causes you to have to use your prefrontal cortex to imagine, analyze, ponder, and even empathize. Consider it an active exercise for your prefrontal cortex.

To make the most out of the "Choose Your Battles" exercise I suggest you identify a few times in your day when you find yourself feeling the need to prove your point, argue your case, or convince someone that they are mistaken—rather than staying open and curious. Answer the questions below.

- How much of your day is spent on these issues?
- What percentage of your day is allocated to this active engagement in judgmental behavior?
- Is this acceptable to you?

Now list all the things you would love to be using that amount of time for each day. Depending on how much time you've spent in judgment, you might list things like:

- Taking a quiet walk
- Listening to my favorite music
- Drinking a relaxing cup of tea
- Organizing my closet
- Working out
- Gardening
- Getting more work done

Finally, to help you embody the idea of nonjudgment you can put more attention to empathizing by revisiting the examples in your discovery journal when you forced an argument even though you knew it would go nowhere good. Pretend you are the other person in that example and based on what you know about the person's life consider how you might feel if you were approached in that same antagonistic way. Congratulate yourself if you come away from this with a deeper sense of understanding both sides of the situation.

10

grace

And she told me a story yesterday
About the sweet love between the moon
and the deep blue sea.
And then she spread her wings high over me
She said she's going to come back tomorrow.
And I said, fly on my sweet angel,
Fly on through the sky.
Fly on my sweet, sweet angel,
Tomorrow I'm gonna be by your side.

JIMI HENDRIX, "Sweet Angel"

Once the most vibrant force in the universe rippling through people and time with laughter and passion, now she lay there helpless and weak—the tempest settling into whispers. Each passing moment was a closed chance for communication, clarity, and physical connection. Her lucid eyes took each one of us in as she scanned the room, taking mental snapshots. My father . . . her pause and expression savoring their six decades together; my brothers . . . her curled up lips likely remembering the way they brought her to her knees with laughter; my aunts . . . a lifetime of shared sisterhood and camaraderie; my cousin . . . infinite gratitude for the niece that would drop everything for her; and finally me, her only daughter . . . a mother's deep gaze to tell me she knew what was going to happen and that everything would be okay.

I held her hand in that hospital bed as she breathed deeply, preparing to speak to us all. She asked me, "How much time do I have left?" My answer, "That is not for me to say. This is your journey, your rite of passage." She nodded and said, "Ok, well not long now and there are some things I need to say." She addressed each of us with a calm acceptance and a strength that no longer needed her volume or wild Italian gestures. She shared her love with each of us, watching us struggle to navigate simple and deep human emotions. I recognized traces of each of us in her lines, her smile, her hair, and her soft words. She had the wisdom of her parents, and her grandparents, as she took advantage of what she knew would be fleeting moments of clarity. She was teaching us how to die and be reborn, the biggest lesson we'd ever know. She was beginning to exist in the space between this plane and that. She was doing her highest calling, role modeling how to find grace in the human condition.

Over two short weeks she loosened her grip on her body-world control, giving up certain navigations to those of us caring for her. First, her ability to stand, then to use the bathroom. Next, her ability to feed herself or find her mouth. Soon, her ability to form coherent words and speak. In dwindling moments of clarity she'd look at me and tell me she didn't want to linger like this. She began to talk of Jesus and Mary and moaned over and over for them to take her home. She mentioned new people she'd never known who were now waiting for her. I held on to each word knowing it might be the very last she'd say that I'd ever understand.

Eventually she lost her ability to swallow. With each growing dependence she drew more and more of us in as we watched and waited on each breath. She saw The Mother and spoke of her. She moaned to us hints of a world we could only dream about. She softened our hard edges and drew us out of petty concerns. She was teaching us how to BE.

She, the most beautiful caterpillar of all, had gone into her cocoon. The Mother told me that her body could no longer keep up with how vast she really was. Very soon she was to wiggle her way out and unfold her magnificent wings. The time was fast approaching when the two mothers, my very own and the one from my visions, would merge and I'd be forever held and guided in my own journey through this human form.

A MEANS TO AN ENDING

Neurosculpting is about molding our lives such that we can expand and make more out of life than experiencing it as an unconscious rehearsal. It is about creating resilience and presence around the natural phenomenon of change. The ability to rewrite one's limiting stories opens us up to entertain ideas and circumstances sometimes beyond our comprehension. By sculpting our thoughts with intention we prepare ourselves to be more conscious in our life's participation. This helps us recognize and savor those minutes we wish would last forever, and make notable the minutes that would otherwise fall through the cracks of our history. In opening ourselves up to the potential of new scripts and new thoughts we begin to sense more wonder, as though we are looking at the world through the eyes of a child, ever learning. On the path to healing and wholeness, neurosculpting becomes our greatest tool.

To be honest, I thought I knew where this book would end. I stopped writing at the end of chapter 9, stuck for quite a while. I paused and wondered how best to sum up all I needed to say in communicating to you about your own gifts of neuroplasticity and healing. And as I pondered the neat little package I'd write, I was suddenly without words. After months of writing and momentum I honestly had no idea why I hit a wall. Then I received a phone call I'll never forget, nor can I discount the eerie synchronicity that it was the anniversary of when my daughter witnessed me flatline when she was just a toddler. I got the news on that serendipitous day in October that my mother, vibrantly healthy until just a few weeks prior when she came home from the gym fatigued, now had less than two months to live. Without any symptoms until this terminal point, she was carrying cancer in her lungs, liver, bones, lymph nodes, and brain. I'll never forget what was happening around me when I got the call: the smell of my friends' house as they were about to eat lunch, the looks on their faces when they saw me on the phone, my utter devastation and numbness as I looked at their small son in his high chair, his face covered in food. I was happy to have their hugs, and desperately wanting to bolt out of there and scream at no one, at everyone.

I was incensed that someone gave my mother—my whole family—an expiration date. Denial hit hard. Not MY mother! How was this possible? Surely, the experts were wrong and the oncology team clearly made some big mistakes. Surely, this was a horrible dream I would wake up from. My mother, the woman who makes everyone laugh, who's committed to cooking and feeding her family and friends with her traditions and spices, who's been a fiery ball of energy far exceeding that of her children . . . THIS woman could not be the woman they are talking about!

The days that followed are a blur of nonstop travel and emotional turmoil. I flew back and forth from Colorado to New York three times in three weeks, rushing to get my daughter there one last time before her grandmother lost all ability to recognize her. We were told the brain tumors would impair her cognitive functions very quickly. Then rushing back to get my daughter to school and normalcy only to turn right around and leave her and care for my mother again. Time was ticking and suddenly all of life looked very different. My life, my friends, my job, my clients, and this book all screeched to a halt and time began to bend differently than I'd ever experienced it.

Gift or curse, my mother didn't last the two months they gave her. She stayed with us for three weeks and died during the crafting of this chapter. Please know that I am using the very tools I've talked about to navigate the most difficult journey I've ever been on, one that required me to hold space for my mother's most sacred rite of passage while watching and honoring my father's most heartbreaking test of losing the love of his life with whom he spent sixty-three years. It was crushing to watch his level of denial as his hopes soared each time she swallowed a mouthful of soup, as though somehow she'd be okay.

So what does it look like to be neurosculpting through the process of losing a loved one? First it looks like a remembrance that we are only guaranteed two things when we are born (which are actually the same thing): all things change and all things die. Yet, these are the two things that trigger us most into our kicking-and-screaming limbic self, causing us to run blindly in the opposite direction. The brain has trouble adjusting to these circumstances as we are forced to let our safe prediction scripts drop away and bear witness to the writing of a brand new story we may not feel prepared for. We battle ourselves as though the left prefrontal cortex grasps in a clumsy attempt to understand and make sense of the infinite, which Dr. Jill Bolte Taylor (author of *My Stroke of Insight: A Brain Scientist's Personal Journey*) describes as living in the right prefrontal cortex. As we rely heavily on our ability to label and define things, we stumble and crumble in the face of that which is undefinable, yet inevitable. I swam in a surreal fishbowl, which seemed to magnify the lens of the here-and-now while highlighting a constant stream of past pictures and moments of reverie. Somehow grief manipulates time and space and forces us to renegotiate our relationship to both of those. I was learning how to dance between the hold of my past memories and the need to be more present than I'd ever been. Minute by minute I watched myself jump between the sweetest memories of my childhood and the way my mother was, and the acute sense of what she needed from me in the present as she declined into complete dependence. My ability to witness this and marvel at it only came through my neurosculpting practice. I meditated regularly through this process, helping myself loosen the grip of fear and stay in my prefrontal focused awareness and empathy.

Being aware of our ability to be thrown back and forth between the past and the present leads to compassion for the self so we can allow for the flood of emotions to come out, as we know this is integral in making space for the new story. My grief, while debilitating at times, was some of the most pure emotion I'd experienced in a long while. Through my meditations the grief had few stuck stories to bounce off of, so it moved through me like huge waves that crashed and crumbled me, but left me space in their retreat to gain my breath and footing again. Had I been holding on to the past those waves would have no way to ebb, and would have buried me completely.

I was reminded of that lens of priority I first began to understand when I flatlined in front of my own daughter . . . *that there is nothing more important than a clear expression and transmission of unconditional love.* It's what we all have to give. I held that as the lens for my day-to-day, and the grief moved more fluidly, more immediately, bubbling up in the moment with no filters or need for judgment and control. In this direct flow I began to recognize the absolute gift of this human condition, which seems to be to get out of our own way, drop our stories, so that we may feel every single moment of this very short lifetime. Those moments of pure presence caring for my mother seemed to last an eternity. They bent time. Weeks felt like far longer as I stopped all the nonsense and poured all of my attention and resources into every breath between the both of us. If presence can make a minute feel like an hour, could even more presence make each second turn into days? Through this unfolding perhaps we begin to experience the infinite and forever.

Each day during the process of her dying I dedicated extra time to my neurosculpting practice and made sure I ate, moved, and slept the way my body, mind, and spirit needed in order to support my own clarity and navigation through all of this. If I were to be petty, even for a moment, that's a moment with her I'd never get back. When I was thrown into a strong resistance around my mother's death, I'd remember that my reaction was a natural expression of grief, but it wasn't necessary to come out in a limbic way that caused me extra stress. In those moments my tools allowed me to yield and set up my own brain and body for a cleaner expression of those emotions, one that didn't dredge up peripheral stories to make it worse. I noticed that certain periods of resistance caused me self-pity as I participated in a victim story. I was able to recognize that my mother's passing was her journey and that the "why me?" attitude had no right to get in the way of her most transformational moment. My practice allowed me to stop being selfish in order to support what my mother needed to do.

• • • • • • • • • • • •

DISCOVERY JOURNAL the death of those you love

Imagine the death of a loved one. If you have had that experience, you may choose the loss of that person. If you have not, imagine the death of a loved one in which you'd feel left behind. In one column labeled "Why Me?" write down the emotions or insights you feel when you adopt this mentality while holding this loss in your mind and body. Notice areas in your body that may tense up or contract during this process. In another column labeled "Ways I Can Support You" write down the emotions or insights you might have regarding this person's death. Notice areas of your body that activate during this process.

Why Me?	Body Location	Ways I Can Support You	Body Location	Mantra
How can my mother be taken from me so soon? Who will I call when I need advice?	Constriction in my chest, tightness in my throat.	I will take care of your day-to-day concerns, I'll feed you, I will put your bills in order and take your stressful chores off your plate.	Warmth in the heart, relaxation in my face.	

Now, create a feel-good mantra that reminds you to step out of the victim or self-pity mode. Examples might be:

- Even though this situation hurts, I know there is more I can learn from this than meets the eye.
- Self-pity is just a limiting choice from the infinite number of choices I have in this moment.

When my mother was dying, I paid extra attention to my actions, slowing down to notice a bit more about all I was doing and feeling. I began to place a higher value on each and every magical moment cleverly disguised as mundane. I saw the relevance of smiling at a loved one, offering someone a glass of water, or holding my tongue to let another speak. When I shut down my victim stories and limbic response I was flooded with these tiny remembrances of my mother's own actions that seemed to embed themselves so integrally in my existence. My prefrontal capabilities became more accessible and I saw my father in a brand new light. I saw a man head over heels in love with his wife who he'd been with since she was fifteen. I saw depths of softness and vulnerability I'd missed in my self-centered youth. I saw that each of his actions was a testament to his and her unified experience. The man I believed was stoic was far deeper than I could imagine. I saw my brothers become caregivers to the woman who took care of everything. I saw territorial borders soften as strained familial relationships evolved. I witnessed the child inside my own mother as she reverted to dependence and jibberish. I saw that all I could do was hold space for her, stroke her hair, and tell her how much I loved her.

The phrases or mantras you created in your discovery journal exercise can help you during the times when the situation wants to pull you into your old patterns. In the case of my mother's passing, I created a mantra to represent the new way in which I saw my father so I could make that a lasting lens. Each time I got impatient with my father's grief process, I repeated the mantra, "My father's strength and dedication to love my mother is sixty-three years old, far older and wiser than I can understand."

I also had a mantra for my mother's departure so I could keep myself from returning to self-pity. "My mother's departure allows her to be bigger than her tiny body could hold, so that she may be everywhere at all times with each of us." I even had mantras to recognize other family members in a new way.

If I stayed in my limbic response of helplessness and victimization I'd never see the magic unfolding before me. My prefrontal cortex was on fire, noticing things about my life I'd missed as I stamped them with a new importance.

During this process of volatile emotions and heated conversations around should-haves I had to pay extra attention to my diet, avoiding carbohydrates and increasing my intake of healthy fats, fish, and walnuts. The first thing my family reached for in grief was cookies and pastries, as well-meaning neighbors flooded us with food. My mouth wanted all of it, but I knew the sugar would not help me process any of what I needed to. I was determined to do my best to navigate this grief and stress from a healthier space. I was learning and bearing witness to how accessible grace can be when body, mind, and spirit all begin to speak the same language. It enabled me to see and respect a bigger picture. There was no higher test for me, no higher validation I'd ever need for the importance of these neurosculpting tools than to have them be my lifeline while I witnessed my mother's dying process from her bedside.

When you really embody the practice of neurosculpting in times of stress or great pain, you will recognize ever more clearly the pettiness of judgment. In my case, I used my own techniques to become open and fearless as I dismantled many of the old versions of me I so easily slipped into with family dynamics. I was able to hold space for those around me in their own fight-or-flight response without taking it on, reacting to it, or even trying to fix it.

It was a tremendous challenge to remain open and compassionate in the face of western medicine protocol in the last days of my mother's life. With full disclosure about what was to happen, we knew she was beginning to experience organ failure in the hospital bed they'd set up in my parent's bedroom. And while we can put down dogs and other animals in gestures of compassion when they are terminal, in New York we could not help my mother in that way. We were not allowed to have her on an IV morphine drip in the house, yet she'd never make it to a facility to get that final morphine dose that could have made it painless. Instead, we were disempowered and made bystanders as she systematically died. In those moments my practice was the only thing to keep me sane, reminding me that I needed to take control of that which I had influence over . . . my own mind and perspectives. I released feelings of helplessness and rage so that the roller coaster of emotions wouldn't lead me away from my presence.

You do not need to process the death of a loved one in order for you to use neurosculpting to help you navigate your most traumatic times. Grief is a great teacher and platform for this work, and it comes in many forms. You might use these concepts to help you navigate the loss of a job and the stability you once relied on. Maybe your loss comes through a move in which you leave behind the life you had created and the friends you made. Fear of change, grief, and loss are opportunities to practice the art of prefrontal awareness and open to deeper healing and wholeness in the process.

In the last evening of my mother's life I had the opportunity to whisper some very important things in her ear, like how honored I am to have been her daughter, how amazingly bright she is as a spirit, and how incredibly deeply she touched our lives. Most of all, I was able to recognize that she was my highest teacher, even in her death, as she taught me about the importance of finding grace.

* * * * * * * * * * * * *

DISCOVERY JOURNAL
limbic moments that limit relationships

Note three of your most limbic responses to loved ones. Examples might be that every time your partner does this one thing, you find yourself using demeaning language and threatening to leave. Or maybe it's that each time you don't get your way you passive-aggressively punish those involved by making decisions you know they'd hate. Your list of limbic responses to loved ones might even involve physical aggression. No one is judging you during this exercise so you can be honest with yourself. Write and answer this prompt for each of those moments: "What would it look like to navigate this with grace?" In answering this question describe as best you can an ideal scenario where you magically had access to an infinite amount of grace. You might even indulge yourself and describe different outcomes based on your insights.

No one prepared me for the layers that were to unfold after my mother's death. I wasn't aware of the crushing heartbreak I'd feel for my father, nor how hollow I'd feel leaving him alone in his empty house. I wasn't prepared for the guilt that arose when I returned back to my own life to tend to what now seemed so small. So my practice and my tools proved to be even more important in the aftermath. I consulted my own brain and tended to its needs as life came back online. I used my own stress management techniques to put myself back together in a way that made life brighter than it was before. You may not feel prepared either for the aftermath of life's waves. But now you have insight into what your brain predisposes you to do, and how best to support yourself during times of uncertainty, instability, and change.

In the absence of stories that have held us tightly and those that have helped mold us comes the space to choose either growth or contraction. Grief is a slippery slope, becoming even more slippery when we choose to meet it with a limbic mindset. Choosing growth doesn't mean we don't feel its discomfort. In fact, I believe we feel it even more when we let it come out freely in each moment it bubbles up. Choosing growth allows us to create a different relationship with grief, and it's in that relationship that we begin to rescript, rewrite, and heal. There is no "one" without "other." Only in the spaces between us lies the potential for learning, growth, and change. We must always be in relation to things and people in order to assign them meaning in our lives. It's time to notice the spaces in between and all they have to offer. Grace presents herself in these spaces.

• • • • • • • • • • • • • •

PUTTING IT ALL TOGETHER cultivating grace

Making the most of this chapter may serve you well in some pretty tough times. To relate personally to all of this you can take this idea of grief and grace to heart and begin listing all the loved ones in your life you'd like to find grace with before they or you die. What would it look like to bring grace into strained relationships? Make a list of all the ways in which you'd amend the rifts between you, if there are any. Examples might look like:

- My best friend all through high school—tell her she mattered to me even when she thought I was leaving our friendship behind when I went to college.
- My daughter—make sure I tell her how proud I am of her.

Once you've made this list, take action on these items. Don't wait until you don't have a chance. In this way you are cultivating grace in the present moment and bringing theory into practice.

Review the discovery journal exercise where you shift your "why me?" statements. Make a list of some of the other areas in your life where your "why me?" shows up. These don't have to be as traumatic as grief. Examples might be when you get overloaded at work, or your family makes demands on you. Maybe it shows up when you are extremely inconvenienced with logistics like expiring car registration, license renewal, or bill paying. You might find you slip into the "why me?" space. Make a list of ways in which YOU can serve the situation differently.

What would it feel like to yield your judgments to neutrality? What could be different if you chose not to react to others' fight-or-flight responses? Who do you need to say "I love you" to before it's too late?

11

putting it all together

There are no extra pieces in the universe.
Everyone is here because he or she has a place to fill,
and every piece must fit itself into the big jigsaw puzzle.

DEEPAK CHOPRA

This journey was intended for you to discover more about your relationship to your own mind, body, and spirit, to explore the possibilities around their infinite capacities and your own ability to create a dialogue among all three. Identifying and recognizing the many different scripts we oscillate between can lead us to profound revelations about the nature of our own behaviors. From here we can take comfort in knowing that each of these scripts is within our own sphere of control, available for us to edit, rewrite, or adapt as each of us chooses. In other words, we can exercise our free will. Neuroplasticity makes this all possible! If we put our intentions into our gift of learning we can harness our neurons' abilities to exercise their domain regarding scripts that work well for us, and prune back those that no longer serve to keep us healthy emotionally, mentally, spiritually, and physically. With science behind us, teaching us how this process works, we don't have to be stuck in an unconscious repetition of life's old patterns. And although the brain is a prediction machine, we know it's programmable and can adapt as each of its predictions becomes challenged by life's curve balls. We are not slaves to our limbic reactions and lenses as we have the power of our PFC to renegotiate old fears as we cultivate compassion, empathy, forgiveness, and the notion that we are all a part of something much greater, together.

This amazing dynamic empowerment can be the source of our unique resilience in an ever-changing world. We have the ability to navigate the vast jungles of our own brains, carving out paths that lead to choice destinations. If we exercise our neuroplastic nature we can shift our own destiny, turning the aging process into a journey rich in learning, growth, and mental engagement. Rigidity of mind and spirit can become a legend we remember when we speak of how we used to be. As we allow ourselves to mold anew with each of life's experiences we embody the very essence of hope. We become alive in the elasticity of adaptation, demonstrating that this, too, shall pass. Each of us can be an expression of the "I can" as we collectively put to rest the "I can't."

As we become more fluid in our adaptability, we can identify and sculpt new stories our bodies hold on to, releasing physical patterns and even disease. As each cell rebirths itself, it can do so from a new and clean code without having to repeat corrupt scripts. We can feed the body with nutritious food and social support as we honor the vessel each of us has chosen to be our spirit's interface with this three-dimensional plane. We can shake off pain and support the healing of trauma in simple ways that help us regulate our stress hormones, guiding us back to homeostasis. Our new mindsets can help shunt resources back to vital organs, bringing our bodies into a richer state of health and healing. Our brains can wire to function with more equanimity. That equanimity is associated with a series of restorative body and brain functions that can begin the healing process for much of our stress damage. This cycle also helps shift the dominance from the limbic center to a more mutual dialogue with the PFC.

This improved dialogue informs our bodies at a cellular level, making it possible for us to choose differently and improve our lifestyle. Our better lifestyle choices impact our genetic destiny by helping turn on or off genes that could otherwise work against our longevity and health. Our DNA is listening to each word, responding to each thought, and in relationship to each action.

Learning to love our beautiful and imperfect selves is another way to gain dominion over subversive and destructive thoughts that eat away at our disposition and our health. This can be a cultivated love that we build upon each day. We don't have to be born with an innate confidence in order to develop it. With practice and dedication we can shed the stories of self-deprecation and judgment and radiate more vibrantly from our own unique expression in the world. Creating links between rituals and thoughts, motions and beliefs, can have a profound effect on how we feel about ourselves. As we recognize that neurons that fire together wire together, we can begin crafting a partnership between our actions and our lenses, beginning with a simple shower ritual of gratitude thoughts or smiling more throughout the day, or expanding that concept into all areas of life. It's never too late to begin this process.

We don't have to be slaves to our fallible memories, putting us in a conflicted comparison with our own selves. Taking the knowledge that memories are always reiterations of pieces of an event, we can begin to place the charge of a memory in its appropriate perspective and move on with what life has to offer us in the present moment. The more we pay attention in a focused way to the present unfolding moment, the more that current experience can become a lasting memory. So if we're tired of what the old memories are doing to us, then we can create new ones with the gift of our neuroplasticity. We can selectively choose what new experiences we'd like to stamp into our neurology and which old ones we'd like to file away on a shelf. The more we use novelty versus fear to our advantage, the more we can do this in a targeted and strategic way. The beautiful thing is that we can bring in novelty all throughout our day with simple and easy tasks.

As we loosen the grip of fear and false memories, we can begin to explore the role of love and compassion. These two powerful PFC-associated states can be harnessed to renegotiate fear and judgment in a way that helps each of us become more expansive. We can save our contraction and fears for when they serve us best—in the face of real danger. The more we step into expansiveness, openness, and curiosity, the more we may have experiences that show us there's more going on in life than what we think we know. Consciousness is not limited to us as humans. This may be a difficult idea for some of us, but the truth is there is measurable data suggesting that species other than humans have complex interactions with the environment we all share. So what more is possible when we open to the idea that there's more of life to learn about and experience than our limited views have accounted for? And if there's more going on than meets the eye, doesn't that imply that some, if not many, of our judgments about others and the world around us are wrong? From here we can begin to determine which judgments about our world serve our greater good, and which undermine it. With our newly acquired practice we can then dismantle the ones that undermine our well-being and spiritual expansion.

We can look forward to a time when all of this neurosculpting prepares us for the most important moment we'll ever know: our own or a loved one's death. The journey becomes an active practice of presence and awareness as we juggle attachments of the past with the reality of all that is temporary. We can bear witness to the ephemeral nature of our bodies, honoring the depths of life they've experienced. We can rapidly shed lenses that have dulled our vision as we take in the brightness and size of our spirit. We can set ourselves up to be in a space of appreciation so that when that inevitable and final moment comes, we meet it with reverence and grace. We are each of us agents of change slipping in and out of the previous and following breath. It's in the space between then and now that each of us has the opportunity to enrich and enliven all of it.

Neurosculpting only begins the discourse. The evolution of the discourse in suturing mind, body, and spirit lies within you and the way in which you dedicate yourself to embodying this work and bringing it into your own communities. Everything we've ever known changes and evolves. Your neurosculpting practice is an important part of that natural cycle. We already know the results when we contract, limit, and grasp desperately for a fixed definition of life. We know this brings us fear, difficulty with change, and resistance to natural cycles of life. Maybe one of your last and final illusions is that there is something blocking deep and lasting transformation, that only *others* can heal and have more out of life. Perhaps this is the most insidious illusion of all. It's time for you to dismantle this story and begin writing your life's purpose.

appendix

daily plan and meditations

Here is a simple daily plan, including a few suggestions for specific meditations that you can use as a template to begin rescripting some of your limiting or fear-based beliefs. This is the daily plan I follow to keep my mind, body, and spirit healthy.

Morning Regimen

1 Brush your teeth with your nondominant hand and think about one of your favorite mantras.

2 Do a five-minute gratitude meditation in the shower that looks something like this:
   a. Breathe deeply with attention for a few rounds, noticing the way the lungs effortlessly fill and empty.
   b. Think of the concept of gratitude. I imagine what it looks like to be in gratitude, I spell it in my mind, and I remember a time in which I was filled with that sentiment.
   c. Assign a color, texture, or vibration to the concept of gratitude and imagine it located and vibrating in the center of the palms.
   d. Wash each part of your body while imagining the color of gratitude pouring out of your palms and filling up each body part.

3 Eat a balanced breakfast on a plate at the table after
   saying a brief statement of gratitude for the food.

Afternoon Regimen

1 Shake for a few minutes in the afternoon to help
   normalize excess stress from the morning.

2 Brush your hair with your nondominant hand
   and think about a favorite mantra.

3 Eat a balanced lunch on a plate at a table.

4 Look at or walk in an outside environment for
   at least five minutes.

Evening Regimen

1 Exercise in a way you enjoy, such as taking a brisk walk or
   a fitness class you love. (You might prefer to do this in the
   morning if it works better for your schedule.)

2 Engage in a nondominant hand gesture or activity while
   choosing a third mantra for the day to think about.

3 Eat a balanced dinner on a plate at a table at least a few
   hours before bedtime. Minimize carbohydrates in order to
   support a full and deep night's sleep.

4 Shake for a few minutes in the evening to help normalize
   excess stress from the afternoon.

5 Shut off electronics or television an hour before bedtime.

6 Do a ten-minute evening meditation that goes something like this:

   a. Breathe deeply with attention for a few rounds, noticing the way the lungs effortlessly fill and empty.

   b. Think of any of your daily stressors. That might be conversations you've had, people you interacted with, or emotions that came up and seem unresolved.

   c. Assign a color, texture, or even a vibration to represent each of these.

   d. Imagine where you might be holding these colors or textures in your own body.

   e. Create a receptacle in your mind's eye in front of you and imagine your body releasing these colors into it.

   f. When you're done, notice if you perceive you've made more space in your body.

   g. Imagine a concept that works well for you, like restfulness, ease, grace, joy, or any other idea. You might remember a time when you felt this, or maybe you focus on the concept and its definition, maybe you even spell it out in your mind's eye.

   h. Assign a color, texture, or vibration to this concept and imagine your body filling up with this as you prepare for sleep.

Here is one more suggestion for a meditation you can use to help you move activity from your limbic center to your prefrontal cortex, and to renegotiate your relationship to certain stories about yourself in the process.

Neurosculpting Meditation to Deal with Fear

- Breathe deeply for a few minutes with special attention to the way in which your lungs expand and contract effortlessly.
- Notice the rise and fall of the belly, the expansion and contraction of the ribs, the way the air feels entering

your nose, and the way in which all of this process is easy, predictable, and consistent

- Spend a few minutes noticing how gravity allows you to sink more comfortably into your own seat. Notice which muscles you can relax with each breath and how much you can notice the way your body makes contact with the chair.

- With each round of breath pay note that you are safe enough, sheltered enough, and nourished enough to be doing this exercise. Notice that your immediate needs are met.

- Draw to mind the idea of a fear that's bothering you. This could be fear of failure, change, abandonment, or any other fear. Take a moment to think of the word *fear*, and then the emotions that come up in this recollection.

- Assign the idea of *fear* a color, texture, symbol, or vibration you feel is a good representation for the moment.

- Imagine you can look through your transparent body and notice where you might be holding this color or vibration.

- Pay attention to the qualities of your body in those areas. Do you notice density or lightness, heat or cold, tension or expansion, irritation or ease, or any other sensations or associations that come up for you?

- Take a moment to focus again on your breathing, which may have changed, but is still happening effortlessly without your need to command it.

- Imagine a container, receptacle, or image out in front of you that can contain the fear you're about to give it.

- Focus on the cycle of your breath, imagining each round helps loosen and release some or all of your body's hold on that fear color or vibration.

- Pay attention to the nature of the release. Do you imagine it to be fast or slow, fluid or chunky, cumbersome or graceful, or any other associations that arise?

- Use your nondominant hand to tap the areas of your body that you imagine are releasing this fear concept. You might even say this mantra at the time of tapping: "Identification, Location, Acknowledge, Release This Fear."
- Imagine your breath moving more deeply into the spaces you've just released.
- Draw to mind the idea of *safety*, envisioning the word and its spelling, then the emotions or feelings you might have if you were safe.
- Assign a color, texture, or vibration to the idea of *safety* that you feel best represents it for the moment.
- Imagine each inhale draws in that color or vibration from its source in the universe. Notice how you'd like to imagine this color or vibration spreading through your body.
- Pay attention to body sensations or perceptions of filling and expanding. As areas of your body draw your attention tap those with your nondominant hand. You might even say this mantra at the time of tapping: "Identification, Location, Acknowledge, and Fill with Safety."
- Move your attention back to your breath and spend a few minutes noticing your body and thoughts.
- Create a name, label, or phrase that sums up this meditation experience for you. And repeat it in your mind as you use the last few rounds of breath to bring you out of the meditation.

Step away from these words and apply what serves you most from this book to your daily routine. After a few weeks come back and revisit your highlights from each chapter and your discovery journal, committing to taking one new piece of information from these pages into your life. Write into the margins any realizations you've had as you've begun applying these principles. Choose one new skill or hobby you will commit to mastering over the next year, five years, or even decade.

I have decade-specific goals that all involve mastering things I've only ever dreamed about. You can do the same and watch yourself become more and more excited with each passing year. What would be different if you could look forward to the next decade in which you learned a new language, instrument, journeyed to a foreign land, or mastered a new hobby? What would life be like if each new decade's birthday was one of excitement and possibility rather than depression and avoidance?

The best way to integrate these tools is simply to use them. Commit to using the following appendices to engage with the **Weekly Brain Changers**, the **Mantras**, and the **Inquiry Exercises**. This will ensure you keep this practice of novelty and observation at the forefront of your day. As a way to help you synthesize and apply all of the information in this book I've created audio programs for you to support you in your practice. You can find great support and application of specific meditations in *Neurosculpting for Stress Relief: Four Practices to Change Your Brain and Your Life* and *Neurosculpting: A Step-by-Step Program to Change Your Brain and Transform Your Life.*

Neurosculpting = Free will, hope, reverence for the body, a healthy diet, responsibility, presence, forgiveness, wonderment, nonjudgment, and grace.

May it be with many blessings that you find a way in which to enrich your life, open to the fullness of your experiences, let go of painful stories, and begin to know grace in this human condition.

appendix

daily mantras
and weekly brain changers

To know and not to do is not to know.

DR. STEPHEN R. COVEY

I designed this section to offer you a couple of ways in which to shift your stories each day. You can use the **Mantras** each day as a simple practice and the **Weekly Brain Changers** as a list of questions or themes you can think about each week. Some weeks you might try choosing a few, other weeks just one. The idea is to read a brain changer and use that as a frame for all of your actions, asking yourself that question in the morning, afternoon, and evening.

Daily Mantras

- I release attachments to unattained dreams and open up to the infinite possibility ahead of me.
- As other situations have come and gone, so will this one.
- This situation simply defines my current circumstances, but does not define me or my potential.
- As I open to the potential of change, I open to new and innovative solutions.

- Real or not, my memories have shaped me into the person I am today. For that I honor their validity, but they do not have to act like scripts that limit my potential from this day forward.
- Even though this situation hurts, I know there is more I can learn from this than meets the eye.
- Self-pity is just a limiting choice from the infinite number of choices I have in this moment.

Add your own mantras here:

Weekly Brain Changers

- What if side-by-side nutritional therapists, MDs, mindfulness practitioners, and science-minded professionals explored the same concepts of self-empowerment?
- What more could happen if we broadened the dialogue around how to cultivate mind, body, and spirit as though they were inseparable?
- What makes your vacation self so expansive, joyful, and full of permission?
- What special permissions do you give yourself when you are on vacation?
- What strips you of that when a random day printed on the calendar notes the end of the vacation?
- How much more could you learn about yourself if you were aware of your subtle scripts?
- What experiences give you the clarity and drive to change what you've always done?
- What inspires you to redefine and rescript that which is predictable?
- Where do you find strength to dive into the unknown and rise up with integrity?
- What if all you had to do was find your power and take it back? How would you use your potency?

- What would it be like to be able to identify a limiting script and simply edit it, or even file it so it remained in the past as an experience you had, but don't need to keep having?
- What would it be like to create a clear communication between all that the body experiences, all that the mind thinks, and all that the spirit is called to do?
- What more could you discover about your own life if you noticed how your thoughts and body interacted and informed each other?
- What could be different about a person's mental healing if the body-world is incorporated as the organ that expresses the mind's state rather than as an unconscious container?
- What physical patterns are you engaging in that potentially reinforce a negative or imbalanced perspective?
- What thoughts are you thinking that are communicating danger and disease to your own body?
- In what ways are you physically numbing to mitigate emotional pain?
- In what ways are you emotionally deadening to mitigate physical pain?
- How are you choosing to hurt yourself to give moments of relief or distraction to what's going on inside?
- What illusions are you buying?
- Are you going to see the glass half empty at that point or half full?
- How easily do you to find the silver lining?
- How well are you there for those around you in need?
- How open are you to seeing another's perspective?
- How much do you have left to give?
- How might you look at your choices differently knowing that each decision can have a ripple effect far into the future?
- What if we knew exactly where our food came from, what went into the life cycle of that meal, and all the hands involved in getting that food to our plate?

- How would we eat differently if we had an in-depth relationship to the food we consumed?
- If you had a reverence for the food you consumed would you waste any?
- What would it take for you to be able to stand naked in front of a mirror and walk away feeling happier and more fulfilled than before you looked?
- What if you could squeeze all the richness and vitality out of your experiences and program that into your memories so that each time you remembered it was with vivid and alive detail? What would you choose to hold on to?
- What would happen to our interactions with others if we cleaned up all the pieces of ourselves held captive by our unhealthy memories and had our full potency in each moment?
- What if we were to take our skill of unconscious programming and make it conscious?
- So what does one do with their own limitations once they find out they are outdated, out of place, and out of time?
- What limiting and fear-based stories are keeping you from fully giving and having love?
- How much better would you feel if after a terrible interaction closing your eyes enabled you to forgive the person rather than continue the blame loop?
- Is it possible for the heart to be in love while the brain is in fear?
- Can we have a genuinely strong desire for connection while still having a strong disposition toward fear, territorialty, and threat?
- How can consciousness help us break free from limiting and reactionary patterns and open to more reverence?
- What if you were to stop hiding behind all you think you know?
- What more could you notice about the wonders of life?

- What if you could put down your expectations and stories long enough to be swept off your feet by childlike curiosity?
- What if in your die-hard grip of data and proof you entertained the idea that it's only proof based on your limited knowledge up to now?
- What if you realized the more you know, the more there is to know and experience?
- What if you stepped out of judgment?
- How are you identifying your battles?
- What would unconditional love do?
- What would it look like to bring grace into strained relationships?
- What would it feel like to yield your judgments to neutrality?
- What could be different if you chose not to react to others' fight-or-flight responses?
- Who do you need to say "I love you" to before it's too late?

Practices to support plasticity:
- Brush your teeth with your nondominant hand.
- Use your nondominant hand to stir things when you cook.
- Squeeze the shampoo bottle with the opposite hand.
- Fold your laundry in a different way.
- Rearrange your drawers.
- Choose a new route to work.
- Hold your car keys in the opposite hand.
- Turn your coffee cup so the handle is on the opposite side.
- Walk around the opposite side of the car when pumping gas.
- Brush your hair with your opposite hand.
- Remember your funniest stories at least once a day, or watch something that gives you a real belly laugh.
- Take a laughter yoga class.

- Have someone you trust walk you around by the arm while you keep your eyes closed.
- Use the nondominant leg to start your climb up or down the stairs.
- Choose a different seat at the dinner table.
- Sleep on the other side of the bed.
- When clasping your hands position your fingers in a unique way.
- Count your money with the nondominant hand.
- Water your plants with the nondominant hand.
- Reverse the order of your morning face and teeth routine.

appendix

inquiry exercises

The **Inquiry Exercises** are similar to the **Weekly Brain Changers** except they contain snippets of scientific information followed by thought-provoking questions to help you apply some of this specific information. My suggestion is to use this section like pulling a card from a deck; each day or week you can choose a note and apply it throughout your activities and interactions. In this way you are creating a real-time relationship with some of the core tenets of this practice. You are living and breathing your neurosculpting practice each time you choose a lens to look through. Over time you can come up with your own thought-provoking questions as this work and information integrates with your life.

• ● •

We have more neural pathways devoted to noticing what's wrong rather than what's right. We build our experiences off these pathways, which then build our implicit memory—the part of us that includes our expectations, models of relationships, emotional tendencies, and outlook on life. Implicit memory creates what it feels like to be *you*. To ensure you build your experiences off what's right about the world rather than what's wrong, it's your job to create and increase your positive implicit memories.

What can you do today to identify what's right in the world rather than what's wrong?

• ● •

The hippocampus connects to our brain's cortex, processing stimuli from all directions. Much of our memory is dependent on this area of the brain being healthy. Unfortunately, the hippocampus is easily damaged by cortisol, a main stress hormone. Once damage occurs we easily lock ourselves into stress patterns and further damage that area of the brain.

In what small way can you take control of your stress today?

• ● •

Novelty and laughter stimulate a sweet spot of dopamine production in the brain that's helpful in learning and encoding memories. Novelty and laughter are also associated with a heightened activity in the prefrontal cortex, which correlates to attributes like compassion, empathy, and insight.

What new enjoyable activity can you engage in today? What one joke can you think about before starting your day?

• ● •

Focused attention to an experience gives rise to neural excitement in the brain and the stimulation of new neurons, even if that experience is just in the mind's eye. As you are careful to put the right gas in your car, so should you be careful to put the right thoughts in your head.

What one negative thought can you eliminate from your mind's dialogue today?

• ● •

Multitasking isn't all it's cracked up to be. Focusing on many things at once taxes the resources needed by our prefrontal cortex, which can only hold a small number of things in its focused attention at one time. Multitasking doesn't mean you can pay full attention to multiple things at one time; it means you can pay attention to one thing at a time and quickly jump back and forth between things. In this way we miss a lot as we become exhausted from this constant toggle. An exhausted prefrontal cortex means we have a diminished ability to access compassion, problem-solving, creative thinking, and joy.

What tasks can you reprioritize or drop for the moment so that you are doing just one thing at a time?

• ● •

The science community is now saying that a daily meditation practice can help depression, anxiety, panic disorder, stress, and even some neurodegenerative diseases.

Which five minutes will you use today to breathe a little more deeply, look at nature, and focus on some positive thoughts?

• ● •

Neurons communicate through electrical and chemical signals using, among other things, ions. According to the Quantum Zeno Effect discovered in 1977, ions are affected when observed. When we observe our thoughts or stories we affect the way the neurons and ions function.

What one repeated thought will you notice today? In what way can you rephrase that thought?

• ● •

Neuroscience has learned about the process leading up to moments of insight or revelation. It seems that meditation helps the brain move from beta waves, which correlate to active thought and attention, to alpha waves, which correlate to brain relaxation. This move from beta to alpha seems to happen just before the brain bursts a gamma wave at a much higher frequency. Some fMRI studies show that gamma wave bursts correlate to the person's feeling of "Eureka!"

Where will you place your small meditative moments today to prime yourself for those "a-ha" moments?

• ● •

Dr. Sara Lazar notes in her TED talk (http://tedxtalks.ted.com/video/ TEDxCambridge-Sara-Lazar-on-how) that in her own experiments, she's measured an increase in gray matter in the prefrontal cortex of those who meditate, and a shrinking of gray matter in the amygdala, which is in the heart of the fight-or-flight center. This is precisely the dynamic that can begin to curb our fear-based tendencies. In other words, our brains are not rigid.

What one fear-based rigid thought will you notice today? How will you change that thought?

• ● •

In one recent study done by scientists at Wake Forest University, after only two hours of meditation training subjects could reduce their physical pain by up to 57%, which equated to similar pain management results using morphine. In brain scans changes were noted in their insula and anterior cingulate cortex—the same areas targeted by pain medications.

In what ways can you take charge of your own discomfort today?

• ● •

By paying attention to your own breathing, emotions, and body sensations throughout the day, you will stimulate activity in the region of the brain called the insula. This area is instrumental in our ability to understand and empathize with others. By tuning in to yourself with intention you can enhance your ability to understand those around you.

How much time will you spend today tuning in to your breath and body?

• ● •

Geoffrey West, physicist at the Santa Fe Institute, notes that a human brain at rest uses 90 watts, 250 watts for a hunter-gatherer in the Amazon, and 11,000 watts per person for the American lifestyle using all of our modern conveniences. Innovation and technology place quite an exhaustive tax on our prefrontal cortex, which needs to consume and then generate more innovation to keep pace. Meditation helps exercise the prefrontal cortex.

What will you do today to bring down your own wattage consumption and feed your head?

• ● •

Technology can be our friend or foe. We can use this to our advantage. What if you were to set your phone alarm to beep twice a day, each time signaling you to take three minutes to neurosculpt and engage your higher-order thought processes? In a very short time you may even develop a reward-relaxation response to the sound of the phone beep. Studies show that sounds accompanying stimuli will eventually be linked to the effect of the stimuli even in the absence of those same factors.

What other daily technology sounds can you create relaxing and positive associations with?

. ● .

We spend lots of time learning how to navigate people, things, situations, and environments. But it's the inner navigation called interoception that can be integral in our ability to heal and be compassionate in the world. The quiet information and stories our nervous system tells us about our inner states can be easily drowned out by the din of thoughts and our outer worlds.

What more will your gut tell you today when you take a few moments to quiet down?

. ● .

If you give the prefrontal cortex the perception that it has control over your stress response it can actually begin taking control. Creating visuals and acting them out in your mind's eye gives your prefrontal cortex this exercise.

In what ways will you use your imagination for purposes of healing rather than judging?

. ● .

The side portions of our prefrontal cortex, called the ventro lateral PFC, control our braking system and help us inhibit behavior and exercise self-control. This area is easily exhausted and uses up large amounts of glucose and oxygen. Exercising self-control in one area may actually decrease our ability to exercise self-control in another. So trying to inhibit or quiet two habits at once is very difficult. You'll be less likely to resist eating the chocolate cake if you'd spent your morning trying to quit smoking.

How can you exercise patience with yourself as you reprioritize what behaviors you'd like to inhibit today?

• ● •

Our conscious mind, which uses most of our brain's energy, actually represents only a small portion of our brain's total activity: less than ten percent. Ninety percent of what's going on in the mind is not conscious. So when the logic mind gets stuck in a rigid stance where you declare "I know this to be true!" it behooves you to question that.

What one rigid belief can you soften today as you question what went on in the other 90 percent of the brain to help create that thought?

• ● •

fMRI studies are showing that when individuals feel left out, rejected, or isolated their brain activates in the same way it does when one feels physical pain. Our social brain networks are wired as deeply as physical survival networks, and are just as important. Community and inclusion are vital ingredients to our individual well-being.

What can you do today to enhance your community connection?

• ● •

As social creatures we all long to feel valued and want to be treated fairly. These are not simple ego desires. These are survival networks according to the brain. During times we report feeling this way our brain activates in the same way it does when our basic survival needs are met.

If you tell at least one person today you are grateful for them, how do you think that will affect your connection with each other?

• ● •

The insula is important in our social brain. It's involved with processing events in the future based on our current body states, and it correlates to experiences of pride and disgust. Studies published in *Cerebral Cortex* in 2012 note that a sense of uncertainty increases insula activity and levels of aversion. Statements like, "Wait until your father gets home" can trigger this response.

What anticipatory language can you notice today that increases your own sense of aversion or disgust? How can you shift those words?

. ● .

Acts of charity have been shown to activate the brain's reward center.

In what ways can you give to someone else today?

. ● .

The mirror neuron network in our brain registers someone else's genuine smile in the same way it registers our own genuine smile, as though we've experienced the other person's smile.

How many more people can you smile at today?

. ● .

The prefrontal cortex responds to each and every small accomplishment by releasing a little bit of dopamine, one of our "feel good" neurotransmitters. Notice when you hit moments of self-doubt, depression, or are unmotivated.

How many of your small accomplishments can you remind yourself of today?

. ● .

The brain can be wired to make us either avoidance-directed people or goal-directed people. An avoidance-directed statement would be, "Floss regularly to avoid gum disease." A goal-directed statement would be, "Floss to have healthy gums." Motivation only happens if we are getting the message in a manner to which we are wired to respond. The avoidance-directed person won't be motivated by the goal-directed statement and vice versa.

Notice throughout your day if you are avoidance- or goal-directed, and begin using that knowledge to motivate you in areas you'd like to change.

• ● •

The business world uses "implementation intention" to mean the intention and focus one puts into setting a goal and next considering all the "if-then" scenarios one might encounter while pursuing that goal. Studies suggest that those who add mental imagery to this have a greater success rate in meeting their goals. If you set a goal to quit a habit you might be more successful if you pictured in detail the many ways in which temptations could arise and the different options you'd have to manage those temptations. Having the script rehearsed in your mind might lead to greater success.

What scripts can you notice today that seem to be running under the surface that keep you from meeting your own goals?

• ● •

Being rewarded seems to activate dopamine so that we feel good. Studies done at the NeuroLeadership Insitute measured dopamine activity during experiments in which a tone sounded shortly before a reward was given. Upon deeper examination it seemed that dopamine increased at the sound of the tone and not at the moment of receiving the reward. When the tone was removed but the reward was still given, there was no dopamine increase. This suggests that the expectation or hope of the reward actually releases the feel-good neurotransmitter. Perhaps it truly isn't the goal, but the journey.

What extra attention can you give to the journey today rather than the goal?

• ● •

Dr. Rick Hanson, author of *Buddha's Brain,* notes that virtue involves our ability to regulate actions, words, and thoughts to create benefits rather than harm for ourselves and others. He notes that those abilities require healthy activity in the prefrontal cortex, and the down-regulation of our fight-or-flight response. When we are in fight-or-flight, we can't attain virtue.

Which neurosculpting practice can you use today to calm the fight-or-flight response and help you attain virtue?

• ● •

The reflective self is said to arise in the brain's anterior cingulate cortex, the emotional self in the amygdala and hypothalamus, the autobiographical self in the prefrontal cortex, and the narrative self in the midline and junction of the temporal and parietal lobes. From a neurological viewpoint, each time you feel like you it's actually a perception built from many sub-systems and glued together with fabricated subjectivity.

If we're assembling the self each time, what attention can you put today toward being the self you always dreamed of being?

• ● •

Because sensory information streams through our cortices with many connection points into the limbic brain, by the time the information reaches our cerebral cortex for logic processing we have already placed

a feeling on that information. It's already encoded as pain or plea-
sure, sadness or joy, love or fear. "Although many of us may think of
ourselves as thinking creatures that feel, biologically we are feeling
creatures that think."[1]

What thoughts can you focus on today as you trace them to their root feelings?

• ● •

According to a study in the *New England Journal of Medicine,* playing a musical instrument and dancing are among the best activities
to reduce the risk of dementia. Songs and melodies running through
our minds give a vivid charge to memories associated with those songs.
The process of listening to and interpreting music stimulates both
hemispheres of the brain in a synchronistic way.

*How many minutes can you spend today listening to your favorite music
or dancing?*

• ● •

Our neurons are decisive and action-oriented. There's no maybe in
their language. They decide to either fire or not, and there's no in-
between. How they decide is a wondrous miracle. Each neuron has
a threshold of stimulation that must be exceeded for that neuron
to send a signal to the next. Each neuron can alter that threshold
based on the situation, stimulus, and even hormonal environment.
Since diet, meditation, and exercise can positively affect the stress
hormones, we may be able to influence our nervous system through
our lifestyle choices.

In what ways can you contribute to healthy neural activity today?

• ● •

Dr. Daniel J. Siegel notes in *Mindsight* that "Given the number of synaptic connections, the brain's possible on-off firing patterns—its potential for various states of activation—has been calculated to be ten to the millionth power—or ten times ten, one million times. This number is thought to be larger than the number of atoms in the known universe. It also far exceeds our ability to experience in one lifetime even a small percentage of these firing possibilities. . . . If we get stuck in one pattern or the other, we're limiting our potential."[2] It becomes our sacred human responsibility to open our minds to more of this potential.

What possibilities could you focus on today if you changed just one of your small thought patterns?

• ● •

We have up to 100 billion neurons in the brain with more of them allocated to threat-detection than to thinking positively. This is why negativity is an easy default and is so contagious. Neuroplasticity promises us that positivity can be trained and exercised.

What one new positive thought will you create for yourself today?

• ● •

The more you think a thought, the stronger that neural network becomes, exercising the synapse, broadening the dendritic reach, enhancing the long-term potentiation, and thickening the gray matter. The thought muscle you exercise will grow in dominance.

What thoughts can you choose to rethink today?

• ● •

Some of our feel-good neurotransmitters, like dopamine, spike far more when we expect a reward rather than when we receive a reward. They can also diminish when an expected reward is not met.

What small, realistic, and attainable goals can you set for yourself today?

• ● •

When we're doing "nothing" fMRIs show the brain is still active in the prefrontal cortex and temporal lobe. Our minds can easily wander to thoughts and concerns of the past and future. Simple tasks like games, chores, hobbies, and activities have a measurable impact on these areas. Blood flow is redirected and the brain can begin to experience a relaxed state.

What new activity will you use to replace your couch-potato time?

• ● •

Cognitive dissonance is our belief in two conflicting thoughts that seem related. An example is "I like ice cream" and "ice cream is bad for me." To justify this we either minimize one thought, or create a third thought to counteract the others. We tend to believe that newly created third thought as a way to avoid the conflict. It's like the smoker trying to quit who says, "I'll stop after this one."

Where do you notice you are lying to yourself today?

• ● •

We need carbohydrates for our fuel and energy, fat for our cellular health and neuron functioning, and protein for building our structures and neurotransmitters.

In what ways can you change your diet to get a balance of all three today?

• ● •

Your brain will work better if you use your resources in an efficient manner. Your brain-taxing tasks that need a lot of concentration are best dealt with when you are well fed and well rested. More automated or mundane tasks can be accomplished with far fewer resources.

In what ways can you reprioritize your mental tasks today to better use your well-fed and well-rested times?

• ● •

Almost winning tends to increase our feel-good neurotransmitters just as much as actually winning.

Where in your life can you stop focusing on your failures and start focusing on the times you almost succeeded?

• ● •

Perceiving life sometimes with an either-or mentality creates a rigid and limiting stance in the brain. Perceiving life sometimes with an *and* mentality opens us up to inclusion.

Where can you change your or *to an* and *today?*

• ● •

A sense of uncertainty can cause us to fear more and project to the worst-case scenario. In the Ellsberg Paradox, groups were presented with a task to pick cards from a deck. Individuals were told that the certainty deck contained 50 percent blue cards and 50 percent red cards. They were then offered another deck, which either contained all red cards or all blue cards. The probability of picking a red card was virtually the same in either case, yet individuals were more likely to take a risk at winning when offered the certainty deck. Even when the stakes are the same uncertainty distorts the way we view life and our potential opportunities.

Where can you identify uncertainty limiting you today?

• ● •

The mirror neuron effect shows us that we map others' experiences to our own internal experience, and the brain perceives we are actually having the same experience. The insula draws up the internal state of the body and maps it in the mind. Perhaps understanding more of what we're feeling and sensing inside can then help us understand what we notice in others.

How much extra time can you spend today becoming acquainted with your body's emotions and sensations?

• ● •

When we empathize, the analytical part of our brain becomes inhibited, and conversely when we are stuck in analysis we are unable to empathize, according to a study done by Case Western Reserve University. Perhaps a comprehensive approach to life is about balance.

Where can you bring in empathy to balance analysis and some analytical thought to balance empathy today?

• ● •

Social conformity has been shown to create false memories in individuals. Group descriptions of events have the power to influence our own memory of the event.

What can you do today to discern your own truth from your peer's truth?

• ● •

The facial expressions of others can trigger our mirror neurons, making us feel what others are feeling. The same is true for our own expressions. Look in the mirror today.

In what ways will changing the expression on your face affect your friends, family, and co-workers today?

• ● •

Rejection and isolation can easily trigger our fight-or-flight center and cause stress in the body.

In what ways, and with whom, can you be more inclusive today?

• ● •

Always considering the worst can predispose us to a fear-based response to the world.

Where can you notice yourself jumping to the worst-case scenario today?

• ● •

The prefrontal cortex regulates attention and thoughts with a vast number of neural connections and a system of arousal and neurotransmitters. If we take no action, our default system can easily resort to negative thinking, which supports a disease state in the body. Each time we perceive victimhood, we favor this same dynamic.

How many times today can you notice yourself thinking, "Why me?" What if you were to ask instead, "How did I contribute to this, and what would it take to change it all?"

• ● •

The fight-or-flight center functions reflexively, with speed and little thought. The prefrontal cortex, or area related to expanded awareness, empathy, and joy, is reflective. It takes time to process, energy to figure things out, and patience to make it all happen. You can go about your day reflexively or reflectively.

What can you do today to balance the two?

• ● •

The amygdala is masterful at creating imagery that's imbued with vivid emotional charge. It's expert in creating images associated with fear and survival. The hippocampus stores these charged stories and references them when a current situation only vaguely resembles the old one. In this way a current event can trigger the emotional charge of a past memory, or of a future concern. At this point fight-or-flight takes hold.

What valuable resources are you wasting on figments of your past, or excessive concerns about your future?

• ● •

appendix

brain basics 101

Axon—The fat-coated channel of the neuron that transmits the electrical signal from the cell body to the end point where it can release chemical neurotransmitters.

Cerebrum—The cortex encompassing all of the lobes, both hemispheres, and some sub-structures underneath the cortex.

Dendrites—The spiny branches of the neuron that help collect incoming information in the form of electrical signals.

Limbic system—A system of brain structures that work together to support the processing of emotions, behavior response to emotions, the creation of long-term memory, the fight-or-flight response, our ability to dream when we sleep, and other regulatory survival skills. Much, but not all, of this system is located on either side of the thalamus underneath the cerebrum.

Neuron—The cells in our brain, spine, and gut that are excitable by stimulation and transmit signals via electrical and chemical messengers.

Neurotransmitter—A chemical that acts as a messenger between the axon and a dendrite, enabling signals to jump from one neuron to another.

Synapse—The space between the end of an axon and the beginning of a dendrite where an electrical signal gets converted to a chemical process.

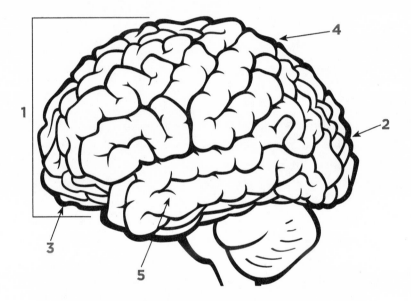

1 **Frontal lobe**—One of the four lobes of the brain located on both sides in the front. This lobe supports our higher-order thought processes of conscious life.

2 **Occipital lobe**—One of the four lobes of the brain located on both sides in the back. This lobe processes visual signals and helps turn them into recognizable vision.

3 **Orbital prefrontal cortex**—The part of the prefrontal cortex above the eyes that is involved in regulating decision-making.

4 **Parietal lobe**—One of the four lobes of the brain located on both sides between the frontal lobe and the occipital lobe. This lobe supports our understanding of spatial relations and navigation, and sensory perception.

5 **Temporal lobe**—One of the four lobes of the brain located on either side. These lobes process emotional content, language, speech, sensory input from the body, and help derive meaning from life's events.

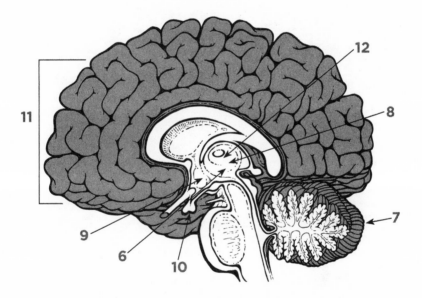

6 **Amygdala/Amygdalae**—This is considered part of the limbic system. The structures are highly involved in processing the emotional context of memories and related decision-making.

7 **Cerebellum**—A structure located in the back and bottom of the brain involved in the regulation of movement timing, precision, and coordination.

8 **Hippocampus/Hippocampi**—This is considered part of the limbic system. These structures are highly involved in the creation and consolidation of long-term and short-term memories. Its name means *sea horse* in Greek because it has a similar shape.

9 **Hypothalamus**—This links the nervous system and endocrine system by way of the pituitary gland and is highly involved in regulating circadian rhythms, sleep, hunger, and thirst.

10 **Pituitary**—A gland in the brain that regulates hormones, reproduction, and lactation.

11 **Prefrontal cortex**—The front-most part of the frontal lobe highly involved in problem-solving, empathy, advanced use of language, motivation, and goal-setting

12 **Thalamus**—A main relay station in the middle of the brain. Both sides of the thalamus are involved in relaying motor and sensory signals between the brain and the body. It's also involved in regulating sleep, consciousness, and alertness.

notes

Chapter 1

1   Eric R. Kandel, "An Introduction to the Work of David Hubel and Torsten Wiesel," *The Journal of Physiology* 587, no. 12 (2009): 2733–41, doi:10.1113/jphysiol.2009.170688.

2   Gina Kolata, "Studies Find Brain Grows New Cells," *The New York Times,* March 17, 1998.

3   Yi Li, Jieli Chen, and Michael Chopp, "Cell Proliferation and Differentiation from Ependymal, Subependymal and Choroid Plexus Cells in Response to Stroke in Rats," *Journal of the Neurological Sciences* 193, no. 2 (2002): 137–46.

4   Kenneth D. Harris et al., "How Do Neurons Work Together? Lessons from Auditory Cortex," *Hearing Research* 271, no. 1–2 (2011): 37–53, doi:10.1016/j.heares.2010.06.006.

5   Moshe Bar, "The Proactive Brain: Using Analogies and Associations to Generate Predictions," *Trends in Cognitive Sciences,* no. 7 (2007): 280–89.

6   Peter Levine, *Waking the Tiger* (Berkeley: North Atlantic Books, 1997).

7 Robert L. Isaacson, "Limbic System," *eLS* (2003), doi:10.1038/npg.els.0000155.

8 Kevin Ochsnar and James Gross, "The Cognitive Control of Emotion," *Trends in Cognitive Sciences* 9, no. 5 (2005): 242–49.

9 Mary Helen Immordino-Yang et al, "Neural Correlates of Admiration and Compassion," *PNAS* 106, no. 19 (2009), doi:10.1073/pnas.0810363106.

10 Nicole B. Witcombe et al., "Preterm Birth Alters the Maturation of Baroreflex Sensitivity in Sleeping Infants," *Pediatrics* 129, no. 1 (2012): e89–e96, doi:10.1542/peds.2011-1504.

11 David Eagleman, *Incogntio: The Secret Lives of the Brain* (New York: Knopf Doubleday Publishing Group, 2012).

12 Patrick Haggard and Benjamin Libet, "Conscious Intention and Brain Activity," *Journal of Consciousness Studies* 8, no. 11 (2001): 47–63.

Chapter 2

1 Kent C. Berridge and Terry E. Robinson, "What is the Role of Dopamine in Reward: Hedonic Impact, Reward Learning, or Incentive Salience?" *Brain Research Reviews* 28, no. 3 (1998): 309–69.

2 Steve Bradt, "Researchers Create Colorful 'Brainbow' Images of the Nervous System: Neurons as Works of Art and Science, *Harvard Gazette,* Oct 31, 2007.

3   Idan Segev, *Synapses, Neurons and Brains,*
    The Hebrew University of Jerusalem (online course),
    https://www.coursera.org/course/bluebrain.

4   Greg Stuart, Nelson Spruston, and Michael Hausser,
    Dendrites (New York: Oxford University Press, 2008).

5   David Rock and Al H. Ringleb, *The Neuroleadership Journal,*
    4th ed. (2008).

Chapter 3

1   Anindya Gupta and Alan J. Silman, "Psychological Stress
    and Fibromyalgia: A Review of the Evidence Suggesting a
    Neuroendocrine Link," *Arthritis Research & Therapy* 6, no. 3
    (2004): 98–106, doi:10.1186/ar1176.

2   Bud Craig, "How Do You Feel? Interoception: The Sense of
    the Physiological Condition of the Body," *Nature Reviews
    Neuroscience* 3, no. 8 (2002): 655–66, doi:10.1038/nrn894.

3   William Jenkins and Michael Merzenich, "Reorganization
    of Neocortical Representations after Brain Injury: A
    Neurophysiological Model of the Bases of Recovery from
    Stroke," *Progress in Brain Research* 71 (1987): 249–366.

4   Paul Gorczynski and Guy Faulkner, "Exercise Therapy for
    Schizophrenia," *Schizophrenia Bulletin* 36, no. 4 (2010):
    665–66, doi:10.1093/schbul/sbq049.

5   Naomi Eisenberger, Matthew Lieberman, and Kipling
    Williams, "Does Rejection Hurt? An fMRI Study of Social
    Exclusion, *Science* 302, no. 5643 (2003): 290–92.

6 Robert M. Sapolsky, *Why Zebras Don't Get Ulcers* (New York: Henry Holt & Company, 2004).

7 Vilayanur S. Ramachandran and Diane Rogers-Ramachandran, "Phantom Limbs and Neural Plasticity," *Archives of Neurology* 57, no. 3 (2000): 317–20.

Chapter 4

1 Terry McMorris and Peter Keen, "Effect of Exercise on Simple Reaction Times of Recreational Athletes," *Perceptual and Motor Skills* 78 (1994): 123–30.

2 David Perlmutter and Alberto Villoldo, *Power Up Your Brain: The Neuroscience of Enlightenment* (Hay House, 2012).

3 Manoj Bhasin et al., "Relaxation Response Induces Temporal Transcriptome Changes in Energy Metabolism, Insulin Secretion and Inflammatory Pathways, *Public Library of Science ONE* (2013), doi:10.1371/journal.pone.0062817.

4 Bruce Lipton, *The Biology of Belief: Unleashing the Power of Consciousness, Matter, & Miracles* (Hay House, 2007).

5 Ian Weaver et al., "Epigenetic Programming by Maternal Behavior," *Nature Neuroscience* 7 (2004): 847–54.

6 Monis Shamsi, Kishlay Kumar, and Rima Dada, "Genetic and Epigenetic Factors: Role in Male Infertility," *Indian Journal of Urology* 27, no. 1 (2011): 110–20.

7 Manoj Kumar et al., "Novel Insights into the Genetic and Epigenetic Paternal Contribution to the Human Embryo," *Clinics* 68, no. 1 (2013): 5–14.

8 Lipton, *The Biology of Belief.*

9 Jessica D. Payne and Lynn Nadel, *Sleep, Dreams, and Memory Consolidation: The Role of the Stress Hormone Cortisol* (CSH Press, 2004).

10 Steven M. Reppert and David R. Weaver, "Molecular Analysis of Mammalian Circadian Rhythms," *Annual Review of Physiology* 63 (2001): 647–76.

11 Andrea M. Spaeth, David F. Dinges, and Namni Goel, "Effects of Experimental Sleep Restriction on Weight Gain, Caloric Intake, and Meal Timing in Healthy Adults," *SLEEP* 36, no. 7 (2013): 981–90.

12 Peter L. Franzen, Greg J. Siegle, and Daniel J. Buysse, "Relationships between Affect, Vigilance, and Sleepiness Following Sleep Deprivation," *Journal of Sleep Research* 17, no. 1 (2008): 34–41.

13 Christopher Gardner et al., "Comparison of the Atkins, Zone, Ornish, and LEARN Diets for Change in Weight and Related Risk Factors among Overweight Premenopausal Women: The A to Z Weight Loss Study: A Randomized Trial," *Journal of the American Medical Association* 297, no. 9 (2007): 969–77.

14 David Perlmutter, *Grain Brain: The Surprising Truth about Wheat, Carbs and Sugar—Your Brain's Silent Killers* (New York: Little, Brown and Company, 2013).

15 Perlmutter and Villoldo, *Power Up Your Brain.*

Chapter 5

1 David Neal and Tanya Chartrand, "Embodied Emotion Perception: Amplifying and Dampening Facial Feedback Modulates Emotional Perception Accuracy," *Social Psychological and Personality Science* 2, no.6 (2011): 673–78.

2 Sara B. Algoe, "Evidence for a Role of the Oxytocin System, Indexed by Genetic Variation in CD38, in the Social Bonding Effects of Expressed Gratitude," *Social Cognitive and Affective Neuroscience* (2014), doi:10.1093/scan/nst182.

3 Donald O. Hebb, *The Organization of Behavior: A Neurophysiological Theory* (New York: Psychology Press, 1949).

4 Ivan Pavlov, *The Work of the Digestive Glands* (1897).

5 Marco Iacoboni et al., "Grasping the Intentions of Others with One's Own Mirror Neuron System," *PLOS Biology* 3, no. 3 (2005): e79, doi:10.1371/journal.pbio.0030079.

Chapter 6

1 Eric R. Braverman, *Younger Brain, Sharper Mind: A 6-Step Plan for Preserving and Improving Memory and Attention at Any Age from America's Brain Doctor* (New York: Rodale, 2011).

2 Lila Davachi, "Item, Context and Relational Episodic Encoding in Humans," *Current Opinion in Neurobiology* 16, no. 6 (2006): 693–700.

3 Elizabeth Loftus and Jacqueline E. Pickrell, "The Formation of False Memories," *Psychiatric Annals* 25 (1995): 720–25.

4 Sascha Topolinski et al., "Popcorn in the Cinema: Oral Interference Sabotages Advertising Effects," *Journal of Consumer Psychology* 24, no. 2 (2013): 169–76.

Chapter 7

1 Diane Ackerman, "The Brain on Love," *New York Times,* March 24, 2012.

2 Bianca P. Acevedo et al., "Neural Correlates of Long-Term Intense Romantic Love," *Social Cognitive and Affective Neuroscience* 7, no. 2 (2011), doi:10.1093/scan/nsq092.

3 Hanz I. Jzerman et al., "Cold-Blooded Loneliness: Social Exclusion Leads to Lower Skin Temperatures," *Acta Psychologica* 140, no. 3 (2012): 283–8, doi:10.1016/j. actpsy.2012.05.002.

4 Thomas Insel and Lawrence Shapiro, "Oxytocin Receptor Distribution Reflects Social Organization in Monogamous and Polygamous Voles," *Proceedings of the National Academy of Sciences of the United States of America* 89 (1992): 5981–85.

5 Doc Childre and Deborah Rozman, *Transforming Stress: The HeartMath® Solution for Relieving Worry, Fatigue, and Tension* (Oakland: New Harbinger Publications, 2005).

6 Marco Iacoboni, *Mirroring People: The New Science of How We Connect with Others* (New York: Farrar, Straus and Giroux, 2008).

Chapter 8

1 Veronique Greenwood, "The Humans with Super Human Vision," *Discover*, July–August 2012.

Chapter 9

1 Matthew D. Lieberman, "Social Cognitive Neuroscience: A Review of Core Processes" *Annual Review of Psychology* 58 (2007): 259–89.

2 Matthew D. Lieberman, "The X- and C-Systems: The Neural Basis of Automatic and Controlled Social Cognition," in *Fundamentals of Social Neuroscience* (New York: Guilford, 2007).

3 David Amodio and Matthew Lieberman, "Pictures in Our Heads: Contributions of fMRI to the Study of Prejudice and Stereotyping," in *Handbook of Prejudice, Stereotyping, and Discrimination* (New York: Psychology Press, 2009).

Appendix C

1 Jill Bolte Taylor, *My Stroke of Insight: A Brain Scientist's Personal Journey* (New York: Viking, 2008), 19.

2 Daniel J. Siegel, *Mindsight: The New Science of Personal Transformation* (New York: Random House, 2010).

index

about the author

Lisa Wimberger is an international speaker and the founder of the Neurosculpting® Institute. She holds a master's degree in education from Stonybrook University at the State University of New York and a Foundations Certification in NeuroLeadership. She has a background in medical neuroscience and neurobiology. She is the author of *New Beliefs, New Brain: Free Yourself from Stress and Fear; Neurosculpting: A Step-by-Step Program to Change Your Brain and Transform Your Life;* and *Neurosculpting for Stress.* Lisa runs a private meditation practice in Colorado teaching clients who suffer from stress disorders, and she is a faculty member of Kripalu Yoga and Meditation Center in Massachusetts and the Law Enforcement Survival Institute in Colorado.

Lisa began her meditation practice at age twelve. Hit by lightning at age fifteen, and clinically dead on multiple occasions, Lisa uses her traumatic experience as a vehicle for transformation. Lisa studied Ascension training for four years with Ishaya monks. She completed four years of psychic awareness training, applying the tools of the Berkeley Psychic Institute, and is trained in Autogenic Hypnosis. She is the founder of the Trance Personnel Consulting Group and Ripple Effect, LLC. She has created and facilitated leadership trainings for executive teams in Fortune 500 companies, the Colorado Department of Health Care, and has worked individually with international management groups. She has created and facilitated Emotional Survival programs for National Law Enforcement Agencies and peer counsel groups. Lisa has addressed audiences ranging from corporate leaders to the FBI and Secret Service. Lisa is a member of the National Center for Crisis Management and ILEETA (International Law Enforcement Educators and Trainers Association). Her mission to share practical and powerful stress management techniques to those in need caused Lisa to develop her Neurosculpting® programs combining neuroscience principles with mindfulness and energetic modalities.

Lisa balances her academic pursuits by playing percussion and dancing in two bands with her husband, Gilly Gonzalez. Together they have brought world percussion into mainstream music festivals, the electronic music scene, yoga studios, concert halls, and meditation centers.

Contact Lisa at Lisa@neurosculptinginstitute.com

about sounds true

Sounds True is a multimedia publisher whose mission is to inspire and support personal transformation and spiritual awakening. Founded in 1985 and located in Boulder, Colorado, we work with many of the leading spiritual teachers, thinkers, healers, and visionary artists of our time. We strive with every title to preserve the essential "living wisdom" of the author or artist. It is our goal to create products that not only provide information to a reader or listener, but that also embody the quality of a wisdom transmission.

For those seeking genuine transformation, Sounds True is your trusted partner. At SoundsTrue.com you will find a wealth of free resources to support your journey, including exclusive weekly audio interviews, free downloads, interactive learning tools, and other special savings on all our titles.

To learn more, please visit SoundsTrue.com/freegifts or call us toll-free at 800-333-9185.

SOUNDS TRUE
many voices, one journey